Isaiah and Wisdom

ISAIAH & WISDOM

J. William Whedbee

Nashville   ABINGDON PRESS   New York

ISAIAH AND WISDOM

Copyright © 1971 by Abingdon Press

ISBN 0-687-19706-6

Library of Congress Catalog Card Number: 75-134250

SET UP, PRINTED, AND BOUND BY THE
PARTHENON   PRESS,   AT   NASHVILLE
TENNESSEE, UNITED STATES OF AMERICA

To David

Foreword

This book owes many things to many people. First of all, to my parents who always encouraged me to pursue my educational goals, I owe an incalculable debt. I am deeply indebted to Professor Brevard S. Childs of Yale University for guiding me through the research and writing of an earlier version of this monograph. In addition, I am grateful to a number of friends who read various portions of the manuscript and offered many helpful criticisms: Professors David A. Hubbard, Rolf Knierim, Roy F. Melugin, Marvin Pope, David A. Robertson, W. Sibley Towner, and Robert T. Voelkel. My secretary, Mrs. Janet Louch, helped considerably in the technical matters of typing the final manuscript; Sandra Whedbee flawlessly typed an earlier form of the manuscript and gave the author constant support and encouragement. Finally, I am grateful to Bylle Snyder who assisted ably in reading proofs and provided unfailing encouragement and a good sense of humor.

Contents

Abbreviations

AFO	*Archiv für Orientforschung*
AJSL	*American Journal of Semitic Languages and Literatures*
ANET	J. B. Pritchard, ed. *Ancient Near Eastern Texts.* 2nd ed. Princeton, New Jersey: Princeton University Press, 1955
ATD	*Das Alte Testament Deutsch*
BEvTh	*Beiträge zur evangelischen Theologie*
BHK	*Biblia Hebraica,* ed. R. Kittel, 3rd ed.
BKAT	*Biblischer Kommentar, Altes Testament*
BZAW	*Beihefte zur Zeitschrift für die alttestamentliche Wissenschaft*
CBQ	*Catholic Biblical Quarterly*
Est Ecl	*Estudios Eclesiásticos*
EvTh	*Evangelische Theologie*
FRLANT	*Forschungen zur Religion und Literatur des Alten und Neuen Testaments*
HTR	*Harvard Theological Review*
HUCA	*Hebrew Union College Annual*
IrTQ	*Irish Theological Quarterly*
JBL	*Journal of Biblical Literature*
JBR	*Journal of Bible and Religion*
JNES	*Journal of Near Eastern Studies*
JTS	*Journal of Theological Studies*

KAT	*Kommentar zum Alten Testament*
KuD	*Kerygma und Dogma*
LXX	Septuagint
MT	Massoretic Text
MVAG	*Mitteilungen der Vorderasiatisch-Ägyptischen Abteilung*
RB	*Revue Biblique*
RGG	*Die Religion in Geschichte und Gegenwart*
RSV	Revised Standard Version
SANT	*Studien zum Alten und Neuen Testament*
SBT	*Studies in Biblical Theology*
StTh	*Studia Theologica*
ThLZ	*Theologische Literaturzeitung*
ThR NF	*Theologische Rundschau* Neue Folge
TWNT	*Theologisches Wörterbuch zum Neuen Testament*
TZ	*Theologische Zeitschrift*
VuF	*Verkündigung und Forschung*
VT	*Vetus Testamentum*
VTS	*Vetus Testamentum Supplements*
WMANT	*Wissenschaftliche Monographien zum Alten und Neuen Testament*
ZAW	*Zeitschrift für die alttestamentliche Wissenschaft*
ZThK	*Zeitschrift für Theologie und Kirche*

I

The Nature of the Problem

The relationship of the classical prophets to the traditions of
Israel and the ancient Near East continues to be a problem
that stirs vigorous debate in Old Testament scholarship. That
the prophets are indebted in some way to their traditional
heritage has long been clear, but the exact nature of their
indebtedness is still very problematic.[1] Unfortunately, all too
often interpretational schemes are crippled by a propensity to
extrapolate too readily a comprehensive explanation for the
prophets and tradition from a relatively small number of
texts.[2] Consequently traditions from widely varying provenances are squeezed into a single, ill-fitting mold of interpretation. At any rate, it should be clear that before any resolution
of the larger problem can be won, systematic analysis of the
different strands of the traditions within the individual prophets is required. As a slender but integral part of this larger
task, I propose to examine the problem of Isaiah and the wisdom traditions. Such a study would put us in a better position
to explore and evaluate the complex nuances of Isaiah's indebtedness to his traditional heritage.

[1] For a good summary of the problem in its most recent phases, see
G. Fohrer, "Some Remarks on Modern Interpretation of the Prophets,"
JBL 80 (1961) : 309-19.
[2] Although various interpreters could be cited, H. G. Reventlow is a
prime exemplar of this kind of error; among his several works on the
prophets, see *Das Amt des Propheten bei Amos*, FRLANT 20 (Göttingen:
Vandenhoeck & Ruprecht, 1962) : 111 ff.

I

To gain proper perspective, it is necessary to set the problem of Isaiah and wisdom against the larger backdrop of prophets and wisdom. In a real sense, Isaiah's relationship to the wisdom traditions has become a viable problem only as a consequence of some radical shifts in the interpretation of both prophets and wise men. Therefore, to understand the dimensions of our immediate problem, it is instructive to take a brief look at the history of interpretation.

Overall the problem of the relationship of prophetism and wisdom has received relatively little attention. For a long time, scholars were content to drive a sharp wedge between prophets and wise men and argued that the two groups shared little in common.[3] Differences of presupposition and purpose gave prophets and wise men sharply contrasting styles. The prophet's word and the sage's counsel seemed to operate in decisively different spheres, with a glaring contrast in relative authority. Moreover, their stance with respect to Israel's sacral traditions varied sharply—the prophet at home, the wise man seemingly an alien. The wise man, it was thought, was secular and utilitarian, involved only in the business of making shrewd observations on how best to get on successfully in life. The prophet, on the other hand, was dominated by a divine vocation which had thrust him into the lofty task of being Yahweh's messenger. That the prophetic books revealed a clash was not surprising.[4] So the prophets sometimes viewed the wis-

---

[3] E.g., compare H. W. Robinson, *Inspiration and Revelation in the Old Testament* (Oxford: The Clarendon Press, 1946), p. 241; J. C. Rylaarsdam, *Revelation in Jewish Wisdom Literature* (Chicago: University of Chicago Press, 1946), p. 23; W. Baumgartner, "Die israelitische Weisheitsliteratur," ThR NF 5 (1933): 279-80; W. Zimmerli, "Zur Struktur der alttestamentlichen Weisheit," ZAW 51 (1933): 177 ff.; A. Drubbel, "Le Conflit entre la Sagesse Profane et la Sagesse Religieuse. Contribution à l'Etude des Origines de la Littérature Sapientiale en Israel," *Biblica* 17 (1936): 407 ff.; W. McKane, *Prophets and Wise Men*, SBT no. 44 (London: SCM Press, 1965), pp. 65 ff.

[4] Cf. Isa. 29:14-15; 31:1 ff.; Jer. 8:9. McKane (pp. 65 ff.) basically centers on this conflict; for a critique of his position as well as our own positive treatment of this problem, see below Chapter IV, "Counsel/ Counsellor and Jerusalem Court Wisdom."

dom movement as a fit target for attack, hurling barbed invectives at the wise man and his wisdom—and little love seemed lost between them. To be sure, the relationship was not simply negative, for the wisdom movement ultimately came under the influence of the prophets as it changed gradually from a secular to a religious movement.[5] Although there are some elements of truth in this description, it suffers from oversimplification. First of all, the understanding of the phenomenon of wisdom has appreciably shifted. Although the debate continues, the picture of wisdom that is emerging is quite different from that produced by an earlier generation of scholarship.[6] All in all, the wise man's

[5] This emphasis on the one-sided influence of prophets on wisdom is highlighted by the two following quotes: "Prophecy alone explains the characteristic qualities and the theocratic emphasis of Israel's Wisdom over against the qualities of the international Wisdom. . . . We may, in fact, define the Wisdom of Israel as the *discipline whereby was taught the application of prophetic truth to the individual life in the light of experience* (H. W. Robinson, p. 241); "Les prophètes atteignent ainsi une clarté et une profondeur d'idées quien la littérature de l'Egypte ni celle de Babylone n'ont atteinte et par consequent ils sont pour les auteurs des livres sapientiaux d'Israël—quant aux idées religieuses et morales—une source beaucoup plus riche que ne peut être la littérature didactique de l'Egypte ou celle de Babylone" (A. Drubbel, p. 427). It is obvious that such quotes are representative of the time when the ethical and moral contribution of the prophets to the religion of Israel was overestimated.

[6] For representative contributions to this changed climate in wisdom research, see esp. the following works: G. von Rad, "Die ältere Weisheit Israels," KuD 2 (1956): 54-72; idem, *Old Testament Theology* I, trans. D. M. G. Stalker (New York: Harper & Bros., 1962): 418 ff.; H. Gese, *Lehre und Wirklichkeit in der alten Weisheit* (Tübingen: J. C. B. Mohr, 1958), pp. 29 ff.; U. Skladny, *Die ältesten Spruchsammlungen in Israel* (Göttingen: Vandenhoeck & Ruprecht, 1962), pp. 82 ff.; H. H. Schmid, *Wesen und Geschichte der Weisheit*, BZAW 101 (Berlin: Alfred Töpelmann, 1966): 144 ff. See also the pertinent essays in the two valuable collections of Studies on Israelite and ancient Near Eastern Wisdom, M. Noth and D. W. Thomas (eds.), *Wisdom in Israel and the Ancient Near East*, VTS 3 (Leiden: E. J. Brill, 1955); J. LeClant et al., *Les Sagesses du Proche-Orient ancien* (Paris: Presses Universitaires de France, 1963). Finally, for good summaries of the most recent phases of wisdom research, see R. Murphy, "Assumptions and Problems in Old Testament Research," CBQ 29 (1967): 407-18; E. Gerstenberger, "Zur alttestamentlichen Weisheit," VuF 1 (1969): 28-44.

stock has risen considerably. No longer is he viewed as a narrow utilitarian, secular, autonomous, and eudaemonistic, whose driving concern was to show how to gain happiness and avoid misfortune. Now he is viewed in a much more positive light—as a guardian of communal integrity, whose place in Israel was as valuable and necessary to the community's well-being as that of priest and prophet. To be sure, though the wise man's concerns overlapped at key places with the priest's and prophet's, his approach was different. His fundamental task was to penetrate into the basic order of the world. "Wisdom's constituent," says G. von Rad, "is this incisive will for the rational clarification and ordering of the world in which man finds himself, the will to recognize and pin down the orders in both the events of human life and natural phenomena." [7] It is on the results of such investigation that the wise man bases his teaching. Moreover, this basic order, which the wise man presupposed, was ultimately dependent on Yahweh, who was its Creator and Guarantor. In light of this new insight into wisdom, the old categories of secular and religious are no longer apropos of a sound description of the wise man and his ethos.[8] An easy evolutionary development in wisdom from the profane to the religious should therefore be discarded.

Secondly, the recognition is growing that the relationship between wisdom and prophets is much more complex than was formerly supposed. This is coupled with the increasing awareness that law, prophecy, and wisdom are not self-contained, isolated categories, but are interrelated in various ways in the history of Israelite society. Hence, it is recognized more and more that wisdom has a zone of influence that extended far beyond the boundaries of the Old Testament wisdom books. Recent studies have underscored time and again the

[7] G. von Rad, *Old Testament Theology* I: 425. Also, see our Chapter IV, "Counsel/Counsellor and Jerusalem Court Wisdom."

[8] For a recent advocate of such an oversimplified categorization of wisdom, see McKane, pp. 65 ff. (For a more detailed critique of this position, see Chapter IV.)

impact of wisdom on Old Testament narratives,[9] laws,[10] and prophetic writings.[11] Moreover, the lines between the functions of prophets, priests, and wise men are not so sharply drawn as once was the case. Although each group had its particular tasks, these tasks sometimes overlapped at key points. At any rate, it is necessary to pay heed to the greater fluidity, and to recognize the complex character of the relationship between prophets and wisdom if genuine insight is to be won.

J. Fichtner is usually considered as the initiator of the recent resurgence of interest in wisdom and prophecy with an article written in 1949 entitled "Jesaja unter den Weisen." [12] He was followed by J. Lindblom who wrote the first comprehensive survey of wisdom and prophets.[13] S. Terrien took the next step in a short article on Amos in which he attempted to argue for a close relationship between Amos and wisdom by showing

[9] See G. von Rad, "The Joseph Narrative and Ancient Wisdom," *The Problem of the Hexateuch and Other Essays,* trans. E. W. Trueman Dicken (New York: McGraw-Hill, 1966), pp. 292-300; S. Talmon, " 'Wisdom' in the Book of Esther," VT 13 (1963): 419-55; B. S. Childs, "The Birth of Moses," JBL 84 (1965): 109-22; R. N. Whybray, *The Succession Narrative,* SBT Sec. Ser. no. 9 (London: SCM Press, 1968). For a critique of the above, see now J. L. Crenshaw, "Method in Determining Wisdom Influence upon Historical Literature," JBL 88 (1969): 129-42. Although this article contains some good observations on method, it fails ultimately to achieve its objective of disproving the case for wisdom influence on the Joseph Story and the Succession Narrative (Esther is a different matter). In brief, Crenshaw fails to take due cognizance of the cumulative character of the argument, though he does raise some pertinent questions at individual points.

[10] Cf. J. P. Audet, "Origines comparées de la double tradition de la loi et de la sagesse dans le Proche-Orient ancien," *International Congress of Orientalists* (25th) (Moscow, 1960) I: 325-57 (inaccessible to me; see summary by Murphy, p. 408); E. Gerstenberger, *Wesen und Herkunft des "apodiktischen Rechts,"* WMANT 20 (Neukirchen-Vluyn: Neukirchener Verlag, 1965): 61 ff., 117 ff., and esp. 146 ff.; W. Richter, *Recht und Ethos: Versuch einer Ortung des weisheitlichen Mahnspruches,* SANT 15 (München: Kösel-Verlag, 1966): 68 ff.; J. Malfroy, "Sagesse et Loi dans le Deuteronomie," VT 15 (1965): 49-65.

[11] See footnotes 12-17 for references.

[12] J. Fichtner, "Jesaja unter den Weisen," ThLZ 74 (1949), cols. 75-80.

[13] J. Lindblom, "Wisdom in the Old Testament Prophets," VTS 3 (1955): 192-204.

stylistic and thematic affinities.[14] Following him was H. W. Wolff, who contributed a monograph to the subject of Amos and wisdom.[15] Reacting against the preponderantly cultic interpretation of Amos, Wolff contends that Amos was more greatly in debt to the wisdom traditions of the clan (*Sippenweisheit*). Finally, the most recent examination of the whole question of prophecy and wisdom has been offered by W. McKane, who essentially concentrates on the conflict between prophets and court wise men, emphasizing the radical prophetic rejection of the secular wise men of the court.[16]

In light of this brief survey of recent research, it is apparent that the question of Isaiah's relationship to wisdom is interwoven with the larger problem of prophets and wisdom. In fact, as we have noted, the whole problem in its more recent phase was raised in conjunction with Isaiah who may be considered as something of a paradigm of the problem. We must now focus particularly on Isaiah in order to delineate the exact dimensions of the problem.

As mentioned already, J. Fichtner was the first to recognize that wisdom's influence casts a long shadow over Isaiah's message and ministry.[17] Fichtner noted that Isaiah employs, on the one hand, several wisdom speech forms, motifs, and terms;[18] on the other hand, Fichtner also observed that there was a head-on collision between Isaiah and the wise men.[19] Hence, Fichtner saw in Isaiah's relationship to the wise men the

---

[14] S. Terrien, "Amos and Wisdom," in *Israel's Prophetic Heritage*, eds. B. W. Anderson and W. Harrelson (New York: Harper & Bros., 1962), pp. 108-15.

[15] H. W. Wolff, *Amos' geistige Heimat*, WMANT 18 (Neukirchen-Vluyn: Neukirchener Verlag, 1964). For a critique of Wolff's thesis, see J. L. Crenshaw, "The influence of the Wise upon Amos," ZAW 79 (1967): 42-51.

[16] McKane, pp. 65 ff.

[17] Cf. also two other recent attempts to deal with the problem of Isaiah and wisdom: R. T. Anderson, "Was Isaiah a Scribe?" JBL 79 (1960): 57-58; R. Martin-Achard, "Sagesse de Dieu et sagesse humaine chez Esaie," *Maqqel Shaqedh, Hommage à Wilhelm Vischer* (Montpellier, 1960), pp. 137-44.

[18] E.g., he cites the following passages: Isa. 1:3; 2:21; 3:10-11; 5:1-7; 10:15; 28:20, 23-29; 29:16; *et al.*

[19] Cf. Isa. 5:21; 19:11 ff.; 29:14.

ambivalence of affinity and antipathy and was especially concerned to solve the problem of this ambivalence. On the basis of the wisdom elements in Isaiah, Fichtner argued that the prophet stands firmly in the wisdom traditions; yet at the same time it was apparent to Fichtner that Isaiah had reacted against his wisdom traditions, as shown by the scathing attack on those enamored with their own wisdom.[20] To Fichtner the best solution for this problem was that Isaiah originally belonged to the circles of the wise.[21] Isaiah's call, however, triggered a dramatic and decisive change. On that auspicious occasion, Isaiah perceived the sinfulness of his ways and his nation's and was thrust into the task of prophetic proclamation. But in Isaiah's new role, he inevitably came into conflict with his former colleagues, whose wisdom often ran counter to Yahweh's will. Isaiah continued, however, to clothe parts of his message in wisdom garb, thus belying his former profession. So Fichtner's explanation for Isaiah's ambivalent attitude to wisdom is very simple: Isaiah was wise man become prophet!

Although Fichtner is to be commended for demonstrating Isaiah's connections with wisdom and hence for opening up a new frontier of investigation, his work is weakened by a number of factors—all of which point up the need for a fresh, systematic examination of the problem. First, his basic thesis —that Isaiah was once a professional wise man—is erected on flimsy foundations. The wisdom materials are important, but they are hardly sufficient to prove his thesis. In Fichtner's reasoning, the fact that Isaiah used wisdom language *ipso facto* indicates that Isaiah was originally a member of the wise. Such argumentation is specious, for it equates too quickly the *use* of language with official participation in the institutional setting of that language. Wisdom is only one of several types of language in Isaiah—let alone the most dominant. For instance, in light of Isaiah's ambivalent relationship to the cult, one could just as easily argue that Isaiah was a former priest.

[20] Fichtner, col. 77.
[21] *Ibid.*, col. 79.

19

Secondly, Fichtner's study is intentionally abbreviated, and he therefore works from a cramped base of investigation. A mere listing of the wisdom elements is not sufficient for a full explication of the phenomena. It is simply not enough to point out the traditional sources; one must also examine Isaiah's purpose and motivation in his use of different types of materials. So it is necessary to interpret anew the specific usages of wisdom in Isaiah. Only when one interprets the particular passages where wisdom influence seems to be present is he in the position to understand the reasons for Isaiah's appropriation and adaptation of wisdom materials.

Finally, coupled with this limited range of inquiry is the fact that recent research renders Fichtner's study inadequate and raises important new questions. There are several areas which illustrate the new horizons of the problem. First of all, in examining the specific passages in Isaiah, one must take into account the research into wisdom that has been done since Fichtner's study in order to do full justice to Isaiah's relationship to the wisdom tradition.[22] Only when one understands as clearly as possible the nature of the wisdom traditions available to Isaiah is he able to interpret with any kind of precision the Isaianic adaptation. Secondly, recent insights into the relationship between wisdom and law have important implications for understanding the prophetic indictments of Israelite society.[23] What is the source—or sources—of the criteria by which a prophet condemned his people? Is it correct, as E. Gerstenberger,[24] H. W. Wolff,[25] and W. Richter[26] have recently argued, that wisdom is one of the major sources for the prophetic indictments? Thirdly, how valid are the connections that R. Fey has cited between Isaiah and an alleged Amos *Vorlage* when judged from the perspective of both prophets' common indebtedness to the wisdom tradi-

[22] See note 6.
[23] See note 10.
[24] E. Gerstenberger, pp. 107-8, note 5; *idem*, "The Woe-Oracles of the Prophets," JBL 81 (1962) : 249-63; "Covenant and Commandment," JBL 84 (1965) : 38-51.
[25] H. W. Wolff, pp. 12 ff., 40 ff.
[26] W. Richter, pp. 147 ff.

tions?[27] As is apparent, these questions take one beyond the point of the mere recognition of an occasional wisdom form or motif, for they pinpoint the problem of the sources whence Isaiah drew the raw materials to fashion the "blood and iron" of his message.

To sum up: J. Fichtner raised an important question in Isaianic research. Unfortunately his contribution is inadequate and obsolete. A fresh examination of Isaiah's utilization of wisdom materials is therefore required. Only then can one more adequately understand this important facet of Isaiah's message.

II

The problem of method looms large in any attempt to examine the interrelationships between such complex phenomena as prophecy and wisdom. At the very outset one runs into the problem of defining wisdom. Since wisdom is such a fluid concept, how can one be sure that a given motif , literary type, or term in Isaiah is bona fide wisdom? Also, how does one differentiate between technical wisdom (i.e., wisdom that clearly belongs to a definite setting like the court) and popular wisdom which is simply part and parcel of any society's heritage? Initially, one must admit the extreme difficulty of achieving anything comparable to complete accuracy and consistency. However, one must still identify the different criteria by which to determine whether or not the language in question is wisdom in origin.

First, it is apparent that the strongest line of argument is when one can show that a given prophetic speech has clearcut parallels in distinctively wisdom texts. Hence, if the speech is definitely patterned on materials that are otherwise found

---

[27] R. Fey, *Amos und Jesaia*, WMANT 12 (Neukirchen-Vluyn: Neukirchener Verlag, 1963) . H. W. Wolff has called for a new examination of the connections between Isaiah and Amos from the standpoint of their dependence on wisdom: "Die Frage der Abhängigkeit des Jerusalemer Jesaja von dem Propheten aus Thekoa kann nur dann befriedigend geklärt werden, wenn man auch an die unmittelbare Verbindung beider mit weisheitlichem Traditionsgut denkt . . ." (p. 58) .

only in wisdom texts, then one seems to be on safe ground in assuming that the speech has been stamped by wisdom. In making such decisions I shall attempt to tap all the relevant wisdom sources in the Old Testament and ancient Near Eastern texts.

Secondly, one must admit that it is difficult to distinguish between technical wisdom and its popular counterpart, for the former ultimately lives out of the latter. Also, the prophet sometimes can operate like a wise man—for example, in the way he argues or reasons—and not necessarily reflect direct wisdom influences. For instance, the wise men had no monopoly on arguments from empirical observation. In such cases, one recognizes that the lines are indeed hazy. However, while admitting the difficulty, I shall still include Isaianic speeches in which the prophet utilizes what seems to be either popular wisdom or a wisdom-type approach. To be sure, it is incumbent upon me to demonstrate the particular type of wisdom that seems to be discernible in the speech. One must be as sensitive as possible to the different levels of wisdom usage in the prophetic message.

Finally, it is necessary to underscore again that an adequate exegetical method dictates that the interpreter not only must identify the types of wisdom in Isaiah, but must also clarify the function of the wisdom materials in their new prophetic context. How has Isaiah altered the wisdom genre or motif to meet the needs of his own situation? What is his purpose in selecting wisdom materials? What are the implications in his usage of wisdom materials based more on empirical observation and argumentation than on revelatory experiences? In short, to understand the encounter between Isaiah and wisdom one must explore to the fullest extent possible the "whys" and "hows" behind the prophet's appropriation of wisdom materials. Only then can the interpreter begin to be sensitive to the depth-dimension of Isaiah vis-à-vis his traditional heritage.

II

Parables, Proverbs, and Related Didactic Gattungen[1]

I. METHODOLOGICAL CONSIDERATIONS

A. THE LIMITS OF THE DATA

A number of Isaianic speeches belong indubitably to the broad category of parables, proverbs, and other didactic *Gattungen*. Owing, however, to the fluidity within the wide spectrum of materials that fall into this category, it is necessary first to mark out as clearly as possible the limits of the data.

The problem emerges initially in speech forms related to parables (namely, simile and metaphor) which crop up repeatedly in Isaianic preaching. For instance, Isaiah occasionally utilizes expanded similes which often appear in the climactic position of the oracle (e.g., 10:14; 17:5, 6; 28:4b; 30:13-14). Such forms have sometimes been used to show wisdom influence on Isaiah and the prophets in general. As J. Lindblom puts it: "The prophetic literature is . . . rich in

---

[1] It is difficult to find an adequate translation for *Gattung*, and as yet there is no real agreement. Some use "literary form," but this is hardly adequate since "literary" implies the exclusion of the oral dimension. Still others suggest *"genre,"* but this too has some shortcomings, for it often implies a more comprehensive category than *Gattung*. Therefore, while I am aware of the problems, I shall continue to use *Gattung* which is gaining a certain currency in the English literature on the Bible. To be sure, one of the pressing needs is for a comprehensive attack on the whole problem of an adequate and accurate *English* terminology for the vocabulary of form criticism which is still too dominated by the German form critical tradition.

parables, allegories, proverbial expressions, comparisons, similes, metaphors. It is natural to suppose that the prophets in this respect were influenced by Wisdom." [2] As general statements go, this contains a grain of truth; but as a working principle for a precise assessment of wisdom influence on the prophets it breaks down because of its generality. The wise men had a definite predilection for all kinds of comparative speech, but to jump from here to the conclusion that figurative language in the prophets shows "influence from the instruction of the wise" [3] is to oversimplify the highly complex forces at work on the prophets. It would be arbitrary and artificial—not to say foolish—to put a wisdom brand on all comparison speech in the prophets. Metaphors and similes are the common property of poets and speakers from time immemorial. One must, therefore, hang a question mark over any facile use of comparison speech to demonstrate wisdom influence on the prophets.

Only when one can make connections to wisdom on the basis of distinctive content as well as form is it justifiable to embrace figurative speech as evidence of the impact of wisdom on the prophets. Also, it is one thing to discern wisdom influence in the use of didactic parables and proverbial speech which display a decidedly wisdom flavor, and quite another thing to say the same in general of metaphors and similes, which are ambivalent with regard to a specific background in wisdom. Admittedly, the lines are often hazy between simile and metaphor, on the one hand, and parable, on the other; for the latter is but an extension of the former. The Hebrews could include these speech forms as well as other types of figurative speech under the rubric of *mashal*.[4] In the last analysis, decision whether a given comparison speech has wisdom roots is determined by the degree of its affinity with bona fide wisdom

[2] Lindblom, "Wisdom in the Old Testament Prophets," VTS 3 (1955): 201.

[3] *Ibid.*

[4] Cf. O. Eissfeldt, *Der Maschal im Alten Testament,* BZAW 24 (Giessen: Alfred Töpelmann, 1913) ; also, J. Jeremias, *The Parables of Jesus,* trans. S. H. Hooks (6th ed.; New York: Charles Scribner's Sons, 1963) , p. 20.

materials. If, for example, the speech includes gnomic truths from the realm of common experience which are expressed in wisdom terms (e.g., as in Isa. 1:3 and 28:23 ff.) , we are moving more clearly in the domain of wisdom. At least, the speech is most akin to wisdom. If therefore the speech contains terms and themes indigenous to wisdom, it is appropriately called wisdom in origin. In short, if a definite wisdom orientation can be shown to be a constitutive feature of the speech, it is a safe bet that the prophet is employing wisdom materials. It is only within these limits or guidelines that Isaiah may be examined for wisdom influence. We must concentrate on what may justifiably be called wisdom if the study is to carry any weight. So figurative speech in general must be set aside because it is not sufficiently clear that it is genuinely wisdom.[5]

Also, I shall leave out material which seems to belong to a secondary stage of the Isaianic tradition. This will include two speeches: Isa. 3:10, 11 (which contains proverbial language about the radically different destinies of the righteous and the wicked) and Isa. 32:1-8 (which is generally considered to be patterned along the lines of wisdom teaching) . Since it is highly unlikely that either of these speeches is attributable to the eighth-century Isaiah,[6] it would be unwise methodologi-

[5] Cf. Isaiah's use of expanded similes mentioned on p. 1. E.g., Isa. 28:4b: the prophet says the "fading flower . . . will be like a first-ripe fig before the summer: when a man sees it, he eats it up as soon as it is in his hand." A. Bentzen calls this "the original short form" of the parable (*Introduction to the Old Testament* I [6th ed.; Copenhagen: G. E. C. Gad, Publisher, 1961]: 179) . Moreover, Isa. 28:20 is a metaphor that looks very much like a proverbial saying: ". . . the bed is too short to stretch oneself on it, and the covering too narrow to wrap oneself in it." As we mentioned already, however, such data are too ambiguous to be utilized as evidence of wisdom influence, although they are highly suggestive and take on added weight in the total perspective of the more distinctive wisdom speech in Isaiah.

[6] Cf. the standard commentaries. On Isa. 3:10-11 see now the careful article of W. L. Holladay "Isa. III, 10-11: An Archaic Wisdom Passage," VT 18 (1968) : 481 ff. Holladay argues that the passage contains many archaisms and may easily go back to the eighth century B.C. This is in sharp contrast to the usual explanation of the passage as post-exilic in date. Although he does not want necessarily to attribute the passage to Isaiah, his arguments increase the possibility that it may be genuinely Isaianic. If so, the case for wisdom influence on Isaiah (or at least on

cally to appeal to them as front-line evidence for wisdom influence on Isaiah. In passing, however, it is pertinent to note that the passages indicate that wisdom circles played some role in shaping the Isaianic traditions in later stages of their transmission. Hence wisdom influence was not only exerted on Isaiah himself but also on the Isaianic corpus.

B. THE SCOPE OF THE EXAMINATION

As just noted, while parables are related genetically to metaphors and similes, the latter in many cases are too ambiguous to be unequivocally used as evidence of wisdom influence; so I do not intend to examine Isaiah's overall usage of figurative speech. Rather I shall concentrate only on more bona fide wisdom speeches. In the present chapter, this will include what has generally been labeled as parabolic speech in Isaiah: Isa. 1:3; 5:1-7; 28:23-29. In addition, I will include Isa. 10:15; 29:16 which have a marked proverbial stamp—thus belying their background in wisdom. Because of their close affinities with parabolic speech, it is appropriate to include them in this chapter. Finally, I shall include in this chapter a didactic speech form which B. S. Childs has identified as "the Summary-Appraisal Form." [7] According to Childs, the form appears in the following passages: Isa. 14:26; 17:14; 28:29. The specific evidence for the wisdom rootage of all the above texts will be spelled out in the detailed exegesis.

II. PARABLES

A. THE PARABLE OF THE ASS AND OX (ISA. 1:2-3)

Hear, O heavens, and give ear, O earth;
for Yahweh has spoken:

"Sons have I reared and brought up,
but they have 'broken with' me.[8]

---

his immediate circle) is strengthened. However, since the passage is ambiguous, it is best to set it aside.

[7] *Isaiah and the Assyrian Crisis*, SBT Sec. Ser. no. 3 (London: SCM Press, 1967), pp. 128 ff.

[8] This is R. Knierim's translation of *pš'*; cf. his *Die Hauptbegriffe für Sünde im Alten Testament* (Gütersloh: Gütersloher Verlagshaus Gerd Mohn, 1965), pp. 178 ff.

> The ox knows its owner,
> and the ass its master's crib;
> but Israel does not know,
> my people does not understand."

Isa. 1:2-3 has the distinction of occupying the lead-off position in the collection of Isaiah's oracles. Appropriately it opens on one of the dominant notes of Isaiah's message—the sinfulness and ignorance of Israel; it is therefore an apt introduction to one of the central concerns of Isaianic proclamation.

Since the parable proper (vs. 3) is an integral part of a larger speech unit, it is necessary to consider the whole unit in order to understand fully the intention of the prophet in using the parable. In many ways the speech is simple: the chief thrust is obviously a bitter complaint against Yahweh's people. On closer inspection, however, the speech presents a number of problems. First of all, how far does the original unit stretch? Secondly, what is the precise *Gattung*? Thirdly, how are elements from diverse traditions utilized? In particular, how have wisdom categories molded the form and substance of the speech? Finally, what is the function and intention of the speech?

1. Delimitation of the Unit

Before the problem of *Gattung* can be tackled, the limits of the passage must be marked off. As is often the case with the prophetic books, the delimitation of the unit is vigorously disputed. While the beginning is self-apparent, the ending is difficult to decide. Many commentators argue for an original continuity with vss. 4 ff., though they differ on how far this extends. Some cut it off at vs. 9,[9] others at vs. 20.[10] In both

[9] O. Kaiser, *Der Prophet Jesaia, Kap. 1-12,* ATD 17 (Göttingen: Vandenhoeck & Ruprecht, 1960) : 5; W. Eichrodt, *Der Heilige in Israel* ("Die Botschaft des Alten Testaments" 17, 1 [Stuttgart: Calwer Verlag, 1960]) , pp. 25 ff.

[10] G. A. Smith, *The Book of Isaiah* ("The Expositor's Bible" [London: Hodder and Stoughton, 1889]) , pp. 4 ff.; G. E. Wright, *Isaiah* ("The Layman's Bible Commentaries" [London: SCM Press, 1964]) , pp. 23 ff.

cases, the argument rests on the grounds of similar themes and catchwords. Some of those who opt for vss. 2-20, however, also appeal to the pattern of the covenant lawsuit as the structural prototype and hence invoke form critical criteria (see below).

In opposition to these views there are strong arguments which clearly favor vss. 2-3 as the original speech unit.[11] First, the meter shifts in going from vs. 3 to vss. 4 ff. Secondly—and more decisively—a change in *Gattung* occurs at vs. 4, introduced by the "woe" and continued by the lament in vss. 5 ff. Thirdly, whereas Yahweh is the speaker in vss. 2-3, the prophet is speaking in vss. 4 ff. Finally—and this against those who argue for an original unity of vss. 2-20—there are clear-cut formal and content breaks at vss. 10 and 18: in the former a new call to attention appears which leads into a "prophetic Torah" (vss. 10-17), and in the latter a trial speech is introduced (vss. 18-20).[12] So the evidence warrants the conclusion that vss. 2-20 are made up of a group of disparate *Gattungen*. Therefore, vss. 2-3 constitute a separate form critical unit and are to be differentiated from the following oracles, which were secondarily threaded together into a catchword and thematic unity.[13]

2. Definition of *Gattung*

The speech breaks apart easily into its component parts. Following Isaiah's opening words, there is a speech by Yahweh which has two subsections. To put the structure in outline form:

 I. Isaiah's Introduction (2a)
  A. A Call to Attention (2aα)
  B. The Motivation: A Messenger Formula (2aβ)

---

[11] For what follows, see G. Fohrer, "Jes. I als Zusammenhang der Verkündigung Jes." ZAW 74 (1962) : 251-68.

[12] The classic studies of both *Gattungen* were made by J. Begrich, "Die priesterliche Tora," *Gesammelte Studien zum Alten Testament*, "Theologische Bücherei" 21 (München: Chr. Kaiser Verlag, 1964) : 232-60; *Studien zu Deuterojesaja*, "Theologische Bücherei" 20 (München: Chr. Kaiser Verlag, 1963) : 26 ff.

[13] Fohrer, p. 253.

II. Yahweh's Indictment of Israel (2b-3)
  A. A Complaint Against Erring Sons (2b)
  B. A Comparison in Parabolic Form (3)
    1. The Analogy of the Ass and Ox (3a)
    2. The Application to Israel (3b)

It has generally been argued that the oracle belongs to the broad category of prophetic indictment speeches. After Isaiah commands heaven and earth to hear Yahweh's Word (using a common call to attention formula), Yahweh himself appears and voices his charge against his people: "Sons have I reared and brought up, but they have broken with me" (2b). Boecker, following Begrich's lead, classifies this as an example of *Anklagereden* (speeches of accusation).[14] A parallel is found in a legal text in Deut. 21:18-21, where it is dictated that a father is to haul an incorrigibly recalcitrant son before the elders in the city gate and turn him over to the jurisdiction of the civil courts. So the roots of Isaiah's oracle seem grounded in Israelite legal practice. In vs. 3 the accusation is expanded and illustrated by an analogy drawn from popular wisdom with a pointed application to Israel.

While some scholars would cavil at our delineation of the legal background of the indictment,[15] no one would disagree

[14] H. J. Boecker, *Redeformen des Rechtslebens im Alten Testament,* WMANT 14 (Neukirchen-Vluyn: Neukirchener Verlag, 1964): 83 ff. Boecker correctly criticizes L. Köhler's designation of the formula as a *"Zweizeugensruf."* However, his derivation of the formula from wisdom circles (following H. W. Wolff, *Dodekapropheten I. Hosea,* BKAT XIV/1 [Neukirchen: Kreis Moers, 1961]: 123) is not overly convincing, for the formula is too widespread to be restricted to wisdom. Amazingly, Boecker does not even refer to the hypothesis of a treaty background in his discussion of the form critical problem of the speech.

[15] There is no need to rehearse the general problem concerning the origin of the prophetic *Gerichtsrede.* Cf. the basic works of the following scholars: J. Begrich, *Studien zu Deuterojesaia,* pp. 26 ff.; E. Würthwein, "Der Ursprung der prophetischen Gerichtsrede," ZThK 49 (1952): 1-16; F. Hesse, "Wurzelt die prophetische Gerichtsrede im israelitischen Kultus?" ZAW 65 (1953): 45-53; H. B. Huffmon, "The Covenant Lawsuit in the Prophets," JBL 78 (1959): 285-95; J. Harvey, "Le 'Rib-Pattern', réquisitoire prophétique sue la rupture de l'alliance," *Biblica* 43 (1962): 172-96; Boecker, pp. 71 ff.; C. Westermann, *Grundformen prophetischer Rede,* 2nd enlarged ed.; BEvTh 21 (München: Chr. Kaiser Verlag, 1964): 292 ff. Suffice it to say that the so-called "profane" origin (Begrich,

basically with what is otherwise a bare description of the speech's form and content. It is only when one attempts to tighten up the lines connecting the speech to the traditional patterns of Israel and the ancient Near East that the real difficulty is met; then the dimensions of the form critical problem become increasingly complex.

a) *The Alleged Treaty Parallel.* Many scholars find the key to the problem of *Gattung* in the initial call to attention and argue that this appeal to heaven and earth stems originally from the lists of witnesses found in the ancient Near Eastern treaties.[16] It therefore has a specific legal function and is to be linked with the call for witnesses. Since it has been "proven" (so they argue) that Yahweh's covenant was patterned on the lines of the treaties, it follows as an matter of course that the prophets' covenant lawsuit *(Rîb)* likewise bears a decisive imprint from the formal and ideological elements of the treaties. Especially crucial is the appeal to natural phenomena: that it is found in some of the prophets and elsewhere is considered irrefutable evidence for the treaty background of Isa. 1:2-3.

Although it is obvious that a full-scale discussion of treaty and covenant as they impinge on prophetic preaching would go far beyond the orbit of the paper, a few observations are pertinent in order to gain a more correct exegesis of Isa. 1:2-3. It must be admitted, on the one hand, that the position has a certain cogency. The parallels between treaty and covenant and hence covenant lawsuit are striking at first look. In particular, the similarity in the function of the call to natural phenomena is beguilingly persuasive.

On the other hand, there are considerations that ought to give one pause before pressing the treaty parallel too vigorously

---

Boecker, *et al.*) seems to satisfy the evidence best, though the problem is by no means settled as yet.

[16] E.g., G. Mendenhall, *Law and Covenant in Israel and the Ancient Near East* (Pittsburgh, Pa.: The Biblical Colloquium, 1955), p. 40; Wright, pp. 23-24; Huffmon, pp. 291 ff.; Harvey, p. 175; *et al.* (See the most recent survey of the data with full bibliography in the article by M. Delcor, "Les attaches littéraires, l'origine et la signification de l'expression biblique 'Prendre a temoin le ciel et la terre,'" VT 16 [1966]: 8-26.)

as the model par excellence for Isa. 1:2-3. First of all, to make two observations of a general character: (1) some questionable jumps are involved in positing the treaty as the original proto-type for the Old Testament covenant in general and the prophetic *Rîb* in particular. That is, it is assumed "proven" that a tightly knit relationship really exists between the suzerainty treaties and the Old Testament covenant, whereas this is not actually the case.[17] Moreover, building on this alleged relationship, it is held as an irrefragable conclusion that the appeal to the natural elements immediately means the treaty background. It should be clear that if the connections on the first level (that is, between treaty and Old Testament covenant) begin to break down then the whole chain of the argument becomes increasingly brittle. (2) The position in-volves an artificial and arbitrary imposition of an extra-biblical schema which often tends to squeeze heterogeneous formal units into an ill-fitting mold. A case in point is our text: in aligning Isa. 1:2 ff. with the treaty pattern, some of the more zealous devotees of the position include oracles of different *Gattungen* and provenances in order to fill out the schema.[18] In so doing, they ride roughshod over clear-cut formal and content distinctions in the material, and flatten out the dis-tinct nuances of the speeches. Therefore, while ostensibly using form critical principles to defend their position, they often violate some of the most elementary ground rules of form criticism.

Secondly—to concentrate on a specific element in the argu-ment—in citing the appeal to natural phenomena as one of the firmest links between the prophetic *Rîb* and the treaties, the diversified character of a general motif in the ancient Near

[17] Cf. D. J. McCarthy, S.J., *Treaty and Covenant*, "Analecta Biblica" 21 (Rome: Pontifical Biblical Institute, 1963) : 152 ff., 172 ff. McCarthy has made some telling criticisms against the alignment of the treaty pattern with the Sinai Covenant. See also Gerstenberger's critique of the deriva-tion of Old Testament commandments from the treaty pattern: *Wesen und Herkunft des "apodiktischen Rechts,"* pp. 97 ff.; "Covenant and Commandment," JBL 84 (1965) : 39 ff. For the most recent comprehensive critique, see G. Fohrer, " 'Amphiktyonie' und 'Bund'?" ThLZ 91 (1966), cols. 893 ff.

[18] E.g., Isa. 1:4-9, 10-17, 18-20 (see above the remarks on p. 28) .

East and Israel is ignored or minimized. Since the motif of heaven and earth is widespread in the ancient Near East (and presumably in any culture stamped by mythopoeic thought), it is quite natural that such a general motif would become lodged in a number of contexts. It is my thesis that the occurrences of this motif in the treaties and the Old Testament represent essentially independent offshoots of similar but genetically unrelated phenomena. Now we must turn to the details of the evidence.

In addition to the frequent appearance of heaven and earth and other natural elements in the treaty lists,[19] the motif crops up in a number of other contexts which illustrate its diversified roles. First, it appears in formulas of exorcism, which are unconnected to treaty oaths. A. Falkenstein,[20] who has collected and analyzed such formulas in Sumerian texts, translates the formula thus: "Der Himmel sei beschworen, die Erde sei beschworen!" Secondly, in the Assyrian *takultu* ritual, heaven and earth along with other natural phenomena are presented as objects for worship.[21] W. L. Moran (to whom I am indebted for this parallel) pertinently observes: "Without therefore assuming any direct connections between the Hittite and Assyrian lists, we seem to have a certain common religious background. . . ." [22] Finally, heaven and earth appear in contexts of prayer and praise.[23] The upshot of all these data is that heaven and earth may be involved wherever invocation of the deified realm of natural phenomena is appropriate—whether treaty-oath, exorcism, ritual, prayer, or song of praise. To limit its locus primarily to the treaty or derivative contexts is to do less than justice to the evidence, for the treaty reflects

[19] See the literature cited in note 14.

[20] A. Falkenstein, *Die Haupttypen der sumerischen Beschwörung*, p. 34. I owe this reference to J. Harvey, pp. 183-84, note 1.

[21] R. Frankena, *Takulta, De Sakrals Maaltid in het Assyrische Ritueel*, pp. 5-9 (reference from W. L. Moran, "Some Remarks on the Song of Moses," *Biblica* 43 [1962]: 319, note 3).

[22] Moran, pp. 319-20.

[23] For a prayer, see the Hittite supplication in ANET, p. 398, where heaven and earth are in the list of gods. In a hymn to Anu, we read: "Great Anu, may heaven and earth bless you!" (ANET, p. 342.) Other examples in both categories could be cited.

only one specific institutional setting in which the general motif of heaven and earth is utilized.

When we move to the Old Testament we find the same broad range of function for heaven and earth—though now in a demythologized setting where Yahweh's sovereignty as Creator vis-à-vis natural phenomena is affirmed. The basic contexts where heaven and earth appear in the ancient Near East may generally be duplicated in the Old Testament, except of course for those in which the deified character of heaven and earth would be inimical to the Old Testament view of reality. First of all, heaven and earth are invoked as witnesses in the context of a covenant ceremony (Deut. 4:26; 30:19; 31:28). Here the closest parallel is certainly the treaty—though this need not imply direct dependence.[24] Then again, Israel's hymnic literature is rich with references to heaven and earth: the latter as well as mountains, hills, trees, etc. are often commanded to rejoice before Yahweh. Isa. 44:23 is typical:[25]

> Sing, O Heavens, for Yahweh has done it;
> shout, O depths of the earth;
> break forth into singing, O mountains,
> O forest, and every tree in it!
> For Yahweh has redeemed Jacob,
> and will be glorified in Israel.

Also, heaven and earth are found in a wisdom context, though probably reflecting an older legal background. At any rate, in Zophar's speech describing the plight of the wicked, he announces to Job: "The heavens will disclose his iniquity, and the earth will rise up against him" (Job 20:27). Finally, the prophets occasionally appeal to the natural phenomena as a part of an indictment or complaint against Israel (Isa. 1:2; Mic. 6:1, 2; Jer. 2:12; cf. also Deut. 32:1; Ps. 50:4). Even here

[24] The case for dependence on the treaties hangs so much on the validity of the general paralleling of the structure of Deuteronomy with that of the treaties. It is obvious that if the whole structure can be so paralleled, the case for the treaty origin of the appeal to natural phenomena becomes very strong. Despite the efforts of McCarthy and others, however, this is still by no means an irrefutable case (e.g., see the review of McCarthy's book by E. Gerstenberger, JBL 83 [1964]: 198-99).

[25] Cf. also Pss. 69:35; 96:11-12; 148; Isa. 45:8; 49:13; Jer. 49:48; *et al.*

the usage does not seem to be uniform. In Deut. 32:1 the appeal leads into a wisdom speech (vs. 2). Moreover, is Jer. 2:12 really on the same plane as Isa. 1:2 and Mic. 6:1, 2? The verbs "hear" and "give ear" are not employed, but rather "appalled" (שמו) and "be shocked" (ושערו) and "be desolate" (חרבו). Would it not be more accurate to say that Jer. 2:12 is a counterpart to the commands that heaven and earth should rejoice (see above)? In Jeremiah the heavens are to be appalled at the outrageousness of Israel's sin; in the hymns they are to praise Yahweh for his redemptive activity in behalf of Israel. These two functions seem to be different sides of the same coin.

In light of the widespread, multiple roles of heaven and earth and other natural phenomena, it appears to be a methodological fallacy to draw a direct line of derivation from ancient Near Eastern treaties to the Old Testament usage of heaven and earth—whether in Deuteronomy, Prophets, Psalms, or Job. To do so is to make a specialized usage of a general motif the source for other secondary specialized usages, when it is more appropriate to say that they spring from similar approaches to the phenomenal world. Similarity does not automatically insure dependence.[26] In short, the commonness of the usage of heaven and earth precludes the single, highly specialized *Sitz im Leben* of the treaty pattern. Therefore, in my opinion, it is much more in harmony with the evidence to posit a common religious background in which the cosmos became a richly nuanced motif. Its employment in the different contexts we have cited is illustrative of its varied and vital role.

To return to Isa. 1:2a, it seems closer to the evidence to understand the appeal to heaven and earth against the backdrop of Israel's own expressed view of the cosmos rather than linking it up with the treaties. One constant feature, which is present in the biblical texts we have cited, is that heaven and earth are accorded a kind of participants' role in Yahweh's dealings with Israel and the world. So the cosmos can be called

[26] Moran's statement concerning the similarity but independence of the Hittite and Assyrian lists would seem to apply here (see p. 32 of our text for quotation).

on to witness the covenant (Deut. 4:19; 4:26; 30:19; 31:28);
to hear a Father's complaint against his sons (Isa. 1:2); to hear
Yahweh's lawsuit against his people (Mic. 6:2); to be appalled
at Israel's sin (Jer. 2:12); to tremble at the fearful coming of
the day of the Lord (Joel 2:10; Isa. 13:13); and to rejoice at
Yahweh's deeds—whether in Israel's behalf (Isa. 44:23; 49:13),
in Babylon's downfall (Jer. 51:48), or in world judgment
(Pss. 96:11 ff.; 98:7 ff.). In Isaiah's usage, he invoked heaven
and earth in order that they might hear how just Yahweh's
complaint is against his people—and conversely how grievous
is Israel's sin. Heaven and earth are therefore portrayed as
vital participants in Yahweh's relationship with Israel.[27]

To summarize: first, the attempt to foist a schema that is
defined too largely by extra-biblical sources on Isa. 1:2 ff.
illustrates the folly of attempting to build a monolithic structure into which prophetic speech is supposed to fit neatly. That
such an attempt breaks down is not surprising in light of
the rich variety of *Gattungen* within the prophets. It does no
justice to Isa. 1:2 ff. to make an artificial schema fit where it
is not indigenous to the material and hence to cram speech
that reflects other *Gattungen* and origins into its mold.
Prophetic speech is simply not illumined by this kind of
exegetical procedure. Therefore, it is necessary to reject the
Rib pattern as it has been defined by recent commentators
and applied to Isa. 1:2 ff. Secondly, as far as the appeal to
heaven and earth is concerned, it is more accurate to understand it in light of the Israelite usage of a common ancient
Near Eastern motif.

b) *The Speech as Complaint.* Ilse von Loewenclau has
given the newest proposal for a definition of the *Gattung* of
Isa. 1:2-3.[28] She has argued that the prevailing characterization
of Isa. 1:2-3 as a speech of accusation (*Anklagerede*) is mistaken. She discounts Deut. 21:18 ff. as a valid parallel and re-

---

[27] In light of this broad and varied role of participation, it is unwise
to be overprecise in delineating the exact function of heaven and earth.
The various suggestions concerning their function in the prophetic appeals
are surveyed in the articles of Huffmon and Delcor (see above note 15).

[28] Ilse von Loewenclau, "Zur Auslegung von Jesaja 1,2-3," EvTh 6
(1966): 294-308.

jects the interpretation of the call to heaven and earth as a call for witnesses as would be found in the legal setting of a trial.[29] Her own thesis is that the speech is best understood as a complaint (*Klage*).[30]

When one evaluates her arguments against the legal background of the speech, they are found wanting. Her rejection of the parallel in Deut. 21:18-21 on the grounds of differences in content and tone is tenuous. The important thing is that the main burden of the accusation is expressed similarly: "This our son is stubborn and rebellious, he will not obey our voice" (Deut. 21:20*b*); "Sons I have reared and brought up, but they have broken with me" (Isa. 1:2*b*). It is difficult not to hear Yahweh's charge in Isaiah against this legal background. Also, von Loewenclau's argument on the basis of the change in tone—Deut. 21:18 ff. is hard and severe and Isa. 1: 2 ff. tender and plaintive—is not really germane to the determination of whether or not there is a legal background involved. Finally, her argument that Isa. 1:2-3 is a complaint because it is in the third person and thus lacks a direct opponent is contradicted by the evidence cited by H. J. Boecker.[31] In the final analysis, she attempts to separate too rigidly between the complaint and the accusation, for there seems to be a clear overlap between the two. In contrast to her thesis I should argue that the speech may still be legitimately seen against a legal background, although this does not necessarily eliminate the characteristics of the complaint which she clearly delineates. Hence the basic *Gattung* in Isa. 1:2-3 seems to be that of a Father's accusation against a recalcitrant son (2*a*), which is then expanded with a parable (3). It must now be our task to analyze the details of the text in order to spell out the implications of Isaiah's interweaving of wisdom language within the context of a legal indictment.

3. Delineation of Wisdom Features

a) *Vs. 2b and the Motif of Sonship.* Before analyzing the form and function of the parable (vs. 3), it is important to

[29] *Ibid.*, p. 296.
[30] *Ibid.*, p. 297.
[31] Boecker, pp. 71 and 84.

note how vs. 2*b* functions in relationship to vs. 3. As is obvious, vs. 3 illustrates and specifies the complaint of the betrayed father. If one raises, however, the question whether there is a smooth continuity between the two verses concerning their respective conceptual and formal backgrounds, varied possibilities are available. Huffmon, building on the alleged treaty analogy, has interpreted vs. 2*b* as "the historical prologue in terms of a family history . . . a manner of speaking that provides a sharp contrast with the indictment on the analogy of animal behavior." [32] To him a basic jar comes in juxtaposing two such highly diverse categories.

This interpretation has serious flaws. First, as argued above, it is specious to invoke the treaty background to interpret Isaiah's indictment. To contrast sharply vss. 2*b* and 3 on this basis is therefore highly tenuous. Moreover, if one invokes the treaty background, the father-son image per se is not used in the treaty itself; thus to identify Isaiah's usage of father/son in terms of historical prologue of the treaty is very forced, to say the least.

In contrast to Huffmon's position, other scholars have made a more plausible case for a stylized wisdom pattern in Isaiah's employment of the father-son relationship.[33] The recipients of wisdom teaching are typically designated as "sons," and the primary demand is for sons to hearken, to obey instruction. The book of Proverbs is laced with numerous examples—to name only a few:

> Hear, O sons, a father's instruction,
>   and be attentive, that you may know insight (4:1).

> My son, be attentive to my wisdom,
>   incline your ear to my understanding (5:1).

> My son, keep your father's commandment,
>   and forsake not your mother's teaching (6:20).

[32] Huffmon, p. 294.
[33] H. Wildberger, *Jesaia*, BKAT X, fasc. 1 (Neukirchen-Vluyn, Neukirchener Verlag, 1965) : 13 ff.; von Loewenclau, pp. 298-99. For a general discussion of the function of the father-son motif in the Old Testament, see Wolff, *Hosea*, pp. 255 ff.

It is likely that Isaiah is utilizing this sort of broad background, as opposed either to the treaty analogy or the mythological view of the father-son relationship. The verbs "reared" (גדלתי) and "brought up" (רוממתי) seem to refer to Yahweh's historical act of creating Israel as a nation, and probably refer to the establishment of the Davidic-Solomonic kingdom. But Israel has broken with the God who has brought the nation to manhood. A parallel Isaianic indictment of the recalcitrance of Israel would seem to add additional support to the thesis of the wisdom background of the father-son motif: "they are a rebellious people, lying sons, sons who will not hear the instruction of the Lord" (Isa. 30:9). Here Isaiah explicitly denounces Israel as sons who have refused to heed the words of Yahweh their teacher. Also, the verbs in Isa. 1:3 move in context of wisdom (see below). Finally, it is interesting to note that in the wisdom text Ahiqar we find some possible parallels to Isaiah's use of the father-son image. To name the most outstanding:

My son, I fed thee with every pleasant meat; and thou, my son, hast fed me with bread of ashes. . . .

My son, I trained up thy stature like a cedar, but thou hast humbled me in my life, and hast made me drunken with thy wickedness.

My son, I raised thee like a tower and said, "If the enemy should come upon me, I will go up and dwell in thee": and thou, when thou sawest my enemy, didst bow before him.[34]

The relationship here is between Ahiqar and his adopted son Nadan who had turned into a seditious rebel, plotting the downfall of his father—this despite the fact that Ahiqar, a court sage, had bestowed the best of wisdom instruction on his son. The pattern is essentially the same as 2*b*: the teacher-father cites his benevolent acts in behalf of his son as a foil against which to contrast his son's flagrant ingratitude and rebellion. Though not at all inferring any kind of interdependency between Isaiah and Ahiqar, the similarity is note-

[34] R. H. Charles, ed., *The Apocrypha and Pseudepigrapha of the Old Testament* II (Oxford: The Clarendon Press, 1913): 774.

worthy and helps perhaps to confirm the common wisdom background.

There is, however, a significant difference between Isaiah's use of the "sons" motif and the wisdom texts'. In both Proverbs and Ahiqar, the "sons" are usually directly addressed, but in Isaiah the sons are referred to in the third person, and the heavens and earth are the direct addressees. Ilse von Loewenclau[35] has noted this difference and suggested that Yahweh is no longer able to address directly the natural hearers, that is his sons who have broken with him. She considers the prophet's call to the heavens and earth as an intentional creation of a new set of dialogue partners for Yahweh who has been deserted by his disloyal sons. This use of inauthentic, silent partners possibly underscores how desperately Yahweh seeks one to hear him, though one cannot be sure whether or not she is over-interpreting the data. If she is correct, this would be in keeping with our observation above that heaven and earth are accorded a participants' role in Yahweh's dealings with his people.

b) *The Parable and Wisdom.*

> The ox knows its owner,
>   and the ass its master's crib;
> but Israel does not know,
>   my people does not understand (vs. 3).

The parable follows a relatively common pattern: an analogy drawn from the realm of observable experience plus an *e contrario* application. The closest Old Testament parallel is found in Jeremiah:

> Even the stork in the heavens
>   knows her times;
> and the turtledove, swallow, and crane
>   keep the time of their coming;
> but my people know not the ordinance of Yahweh
>   (Jer. 8:7).

---

[35] Ilse von Loewenclau, p. 304.

We might also add as an example the New Testament saying:

... You know how to interpret the appearance of earth and sky; but why do you not know how to interpret the present time? (Luke 12:56) [36]

Like the wise men, Isaiah and Jeremiah discern an affinity between two seemingly disparate realms. The proverbial stamp of vs. 3a is self-apparent and belies the pedagogical interests of the speech. The picture of animal behavior is common in wisdom, for the sages often had recourse to the animal kingdom to draw analogies for their lessons.[37] Moreover, the ass and ox frequently appear in ancient Near Eastern wisdom; from the earliest times both were favorite subjects for makers of proverbs and were known especially for their stupidity and streaks of contrariness.[38] For example, the stupid man who is seduced by a harlot is likened to an ox:

> All at once he follows her,
> as an ox goes to the slaughter,
> ...
> he does not know it will
> cost him his life (Prov. 7:22a, 23b).

In another place the fool is compared with an ass:

> A whip for the horse, a bridle for the ass, and
> a rod for the back of fools (Prov. 26:3).

However, Isaiah's use of the ass and ox motif goes against the normal wisdom tradition and is particularly apt, for the effectiveness of their being set in a positive light to contrast with Israel's behavior is heightened when one thinks of the characteristics customarily assigned to them. Even when compared

[36] For further examples, see R. Bultmann, *History of the Synoptic Tradition*, trans. from the third German ed. with supplementary material by J. Marsh (New York: Harper & Row, 1963), p. 185.

[37] Cf. I Kings 4:33; Prov. 6:6 ff.; 7:22; 14:4; 26:3; 30:24 ff.; Sir. 11:20; 26:7; 27:9-10; 30:8; 33:4, 6; and many others.

[38] Cf. the collection of ass/ox proverbs in E. I. Gordon, *Sumerian Proverbs: Glimpses of Everyday Life in Ancient Mesopotamia* (University of Pennsylvania, Philadelphia: The University Museum, 1959), pp. 230 ff.

with stupid animals, Israel comes off a poor second; the ironic implication is painfully clear.

The analogy of the ass and ox serves to display nakedly the unnatural side of Israel's stupidity, as does Isaiah's use of the metaphor of disobedient sons. The ass/ox metaphor is very much like Jeremiah's example of the birds that know the times of their coming—in contrast to Israel's ignorance. In both cases Isaiah and Jeremiah, like the wise men, show an awareness of a basic order within the phenomenal world on which they draw to put across a fearful lesson.[39] Isaiah can depict Israel's sinfulness in terms of a breakdown in the basic order of the world. Israel's behavior is anything but wise; in fact, it does not even measure up to the behavior one can expect from stupid animals. To be sure, Isaiah transposes the wisdom understanding of the world into a special key, for he portrays the basic order in terms of the Yahweh-Israel bond. The important matter, however, is that Isaiah characterizes the Yahweh-Israel bond according to wisdom categories; like the wise men, Isaiah can see a fundamental continuity in the different structures of the basic order of the world.[40] Isaiah's parable, then, has more significance than mere ornamentation; it evidences a constitutive value for a chief facet of his message, focusing on the fundamental structure of reality to which he appeals. Against this background, his intention is to highlight the blatant unnaturalness of Israel's sins.

Again, it is within a wisdom context that the verbs ידע ("know") and התבונן ("understand") are best understood. In contrast, W. Zimmerli[41] has suggested that "knowledge" here is to be seen on the same line as the "knowledge of God" so central to Hosea. In saying this, however, he fails to take note

---

[39] Recent studies in ancient Near Eastern wisdom have increasingly emphasized how the wise men concentrated on this basic order; e.g., see Gese, *Lehre und Wirklichkeit in der alten Weisheit*, pp. 11 ff. and 33 ff.; von Rad, *Old Testament Theology* I: 421 ff.

[40] I am partially indebted to Wildberger (pp. 14-15) for my interpretation.

[41] W. Zimmerli, *The Law and the Prophets*, trans. R. E. Clements (Oxford: Basil Blackwell, 1965), p. 74.

of the wisdom background, for a similar usage of the two verbs is amply attested in wisdom texts.[42]

It is significant that the two verbs have no object. The Septuagint attempts to rectify this by adding "me" as the direct object. It is wiser, however, to stick with the Massoretic Text. In my judgment, the lack of object is intentional and gives insight into the nature of wisdom and knowledge in this context. In contrast to the ass and ox, Israel has lost her way; she no longer has a sense of direction; in short, she has lost touch with reality. To Isaiah, then, true wisdom may be defined thus: "to know where I belong, to know whose voice is valid for me." [43] Hence Isaiah intentionally leaves the verbs without an object, and by so doing emphasizes the utter loss of insight and understanding on Israel's part. From the perspective of the basic order of reality conditioned by the long history of the Yahweh-Israel relationship, Israel has suffered an astounding loss of knowledge. For Isaiah, as Wildberger rightly emphasizes, there is no sharp contrast between the wisdom ideal—insightful, knowledgeable conduct—and the demand of loyalty within the Yahweh-Israel relationship.[44] So Isaiah defines Israel's lack of filial loyalty in terms of a breakdown and failure of wisdom.

To conclude: coming on the heels of the opening call to heaven and earth, the two indictments in vss. 2b and 3 show the rich complexity of Isaiah's language. Here he skillfully places two different genres—legal complaint and didactic parable—and two different metaphors—father/son and ass/ox— in a back-to-back position; yet at the same time he implies an inner affinity between the two. First of all, both have wisdom

[42] The verb (ידע) of course is too widespread to be limited to one specific context and hence its background must be determined from case to case; but the evidence for התבגן points unmistakably to a background in wisdom (cf. Pss. 27:10; 107:43; 119:95, 100, 104; Job 11:11; 23:15; 26:14; 30:20; 31:1; 32:12; 37:14; 38:18). Also, as Wildberger notes, the intransitive use of the verbs is decisive for wisdom (p. 15). Finally, the proverbial stamp of the speech would seem to make the wisdom background self-evident.

[43] Ilse von Loewenclau, p. 307.

[44] Wildberger, p. 15.

characteristics: the father/son imagery and the parable of the ass and ox. Secondly, there is a certain affinity between the two metaphors: both depend on imagery drawn from domestic life. Yahweh had "reared and brought up" Israel as his son, hence implying his redemptive acts in Israel's behalf by which she was constituted a nation with a homeland; but Israel had "broken with" (פשע) Yahweh, had run away from her Father's house, and was worse than domesticated animals—the ass and ox—which at least knew their owner and their home.[45] The "sons" lacked the wisdom of beasts of burden. Moreover, both metaphors serve to underscore the unnaturalness of Israel's behavior; her disobedience was a blatant failure in light of natural expectations. It is indeed striking how Isaiah has deftly intertwined his basic indictment of Israel with stylized wisdom patterns. The passage is an impressive example of the variety of language Isaiah can tap for his message.

B. THE PARABLE OF THE VINEYARD (ISA. 5:1-7)

Let me sing for my friend,
a love song of his vineyard.
My friend had a vineyard,
on a very fertile hill.
He dug it, cleared it of stones,
and planted it with the best vines.
In the middle he built a watchtower,
and also hewed out a wine vat.
He expected it to produce grapes,
but it produced sour grapes,
And now, inhabitants of Jerusalem,
and men of Judah,
Judge, I ask, between me and my vineyard.
What else could I have done for my vineyard,
that I have not done?
I expected it to produce grapes;
Why did it produce sour grapes?
And now I will tell you what
I am going to do to my vineyard:
I will remove its hedge that it be devoured;
I will rip down its wall that it be trampled down.

[45] I am dependent for this interpretation of the meaning of פשע on R. Knierim, p. 180.

I will lay it waste; it will not be pruned or hoed,
and briars and thorns will spring up.
I will command the clouds to rain no rain upon it.
For the vineyard of Yahweh of hosts is the house of Israel,
and the men of Judah are his choice plant.
He expected justice, but behold bloodshed;
righteousness, but behold a cry.

The famous "Parable of the Vineyard" [46]—surely one of the most artistic passages in the Bible—is a classic illustration of Isaiah's inimitable style. And it is a testimony of his use of wisdom style and techniques; for it is an outstanding embodiment of the parabolic form which Isaiah adapts for his own purpose.

1. Delimitation of the Unit

That Isa. 5:1-7 is a well-cut piece of literature is transparently clear. Sharply set off from the preceding and following sections, it is an independent, artistic unity, replete with introduction (1a), body (1b-6) and conclusion (7). The jarring changes of pace (e.g., the shifts in speakers) [47] plus the element of surprise and constantly shifting perspective, are built into the basic structure and help to heighten the overall effectiveness.

The structure is fairly easy to describe, with clear signals in the text. The prophet leads off with a request for attention (vs. 1a) in which he introduces his topic—a song of love. Next comes the actual presentation of the song, which concerns a man's disappointment with his vineyard (vss. 1b-2). The first major break comes between vss. 2 and 3, and the second main unit is comprised by the speech of the owner (vss. 3-6). A ועתה ("and now") alerts one to the break, which is confirmed by the shifts of speakers (from the prophet to the owner) and the change in genre (from love poetry to legal proceedings). Another ועתה ("and now") introduces the second part of the owner's speech (vss. 5-6), where punishment is announced for the worthless vineyard. The direct applica-

---

[46] The vineyard is a favorite symbol in the Bible for Israel (cf. Hos. 10:11; Ps. 80; Isa. 27:1 ff.; Matt. 21:33 ff.).

[47] Note also the change in meter.

44

tion to Israel appears in vs. 7. Here the scene shifts back to the phophet, who equates Israel with the vineyard and then exits with a striking summation of the reason for Yahweh's disappointment in Israel, utilizing a well-turned wordplay.[48] An outline puts the structure in clearest form:

I. The Request for Attention (vs. 1*a*)
II. The Recital of a Love Song (vss. 1*b*-2)
III. The Speech of the Owner (vss. 3-6)
    A. ועתה: First Subsection: (vss. 3-4)
        1. A Demand for Decision (vs. 3)
        2. A Self-vindicating Question (vs. 4)
    B. ועתה: Second Subsection: Announcement of Punishment for Vineyard (vss. 5-6)
IV. The Statement of Application (vs. 7)
    A. The Equation of Israel with the Vineyard (vs. 7*a*)
    B. The Epitome of the Problem (vs. 7*b*)

2. Definition of *Gattung*

The definition of the *Gattung* in Isa. 5:1-7 has had much debate—marked often unfortunately by some outlandish speculation.[49] Though it is not needful to rehearse the vagaries of the various approaches, it is important to delineate in general the nature and type of the individual formal elements and the basic *Gattung*.

That the first two verses follow the pattern of a love song seems obvious, although the point has not gone unchallenged. Whether the *whole* unit, however, is formally a song is another question. A. Bentzen labels the whole poem a song of a disappointed lover and interprets it in allegorical terms.[50] So, for example, vss. 5-6 contain a curse of childlessness hurled against the faithless wife, which in turn becomes a curse leveled against

[48] משפט משפח צדקה צעקה. The attempts to bring these puns over into English have generally fallen flat (cf. the commentaries) .
[49] Cf. the following articles for a history of recent interpretations: H. Junker, "Die literarische Art von Jes. 5, 1-7," *Biblica* 40 (1959) : 259-66; P. de Orbiso, "El cántico a la viña del amado Is. 5, 1-7," *Estudios Eclesiásticos* 34 (1960) : 715-31.
[50] A. Bentzen, "Zur Erläuterung von Jes. 5, 1-7," *AFO* 4 (1927) : 209-10.

Israel. Now to be sure, the "vineyard" often is used as a symbolic term to designate the loved one.[51] Hence, that the hearers would have interpreted the song as telling a love story is most probable. However, whether one can interpret the whole as an allegory is problematic. In my opinion, Bentzen's analysis blurs some of the clear-cut form critical distinctions within the text—distinctions which do not appear in sharp focus when seen from the flat perspective of the single *Gattung* of a love song. First, there is the change in speakers at vss. 3 ff., where the "I" of the owner enters the picture. Moreover, a third party—the men of Jerusalem and Judah—is called on to render a decision in the case; so the listeners become participants. This signals a radical change in form: we are transferred from the world of love poetry to that of legal proceedings. As H. J. Boecker has ably shown, vss. 3-6 have a firm setting in Israel's legal life.[52] Vs. 3 itself is "an introductory formula with which the plaintiff turns to the court and demands it to come to a legal decision in the case that is laid before it." [53] So vss. 3 ff., while continuing the image of the vineyard, alter the perspective—court is now in session. Vs. 4 in turn brings the charge in the form of a question to the court, placing it before the "compulsion of an answer." [54] Once again the perspective shifts in vss. 5-6 (though we are still in the midst of legal proceedings) and the accuser turns judge, announcing the sentence of doom.

By ignoring these formal differences, Bentzen is guilty of absolutizing one formal category (that of love song) and reading the whole speech from a faulty perspective. He compounds his error by interpreting the speech according to allegorical principles, which go beyond what the text actually says. Also, while he recognizes the special prophetic usage of the speech (as shown by the application in vs. 7), he fails to see how the prior legal elements have received a prophetic adaptation. In Isaiah's appropriation of judicial forms, he

[51] Cf. Song of Solomon 1:6; 2:15; 8:1-2.
[52] Boecker, pp. 81 ff.
[53] *Ibid.*, p. 82.
[54] Begrich, *Studien zu Deuterojesaia,* p. 34 (quoted by Boecker, p. 82).

follows the invective-threat pattern of a prophetic judgment speech. Thus the sin of Israel is laid bare, and the sentence of judgment announced—both in modified legal terms.

In contrast to Bentzen's allegorical interpretation, it is more accurate to see the heterogeneous formal elements as subordinate parts of a parable. Both the love song and the legal speech become elements of a carefully constructed parable, which in turn functions as a prophetic judgment speech.[55] So it can be rightly called a "juridical parable." [56] The parabolic form and the vineyard imagery are the glue that holds the diverse parts together, giving the whole speech a cohesive unity.

To show more clearly the parabolic nature of the speech one needs only to compare Nathan's well-known parable.[57] First, instead of Isaiah's love song—though corresponding to it functionally—Nathan employs a story in narrative form (II Sam. 12:1b-4), which is a common parabolic technique used often by Jesus. Also, in both speeches the hearer's judgment is elicited—which unbeknown to him has the boomerang effect of turning the judgment back on his own head. Lastly, in each instance the prophet applies the word explicitly to the hearer(s) (II Sam. 12:7 and Isa. 5:7). It is evident, then, that both speeches, while containing varied formal elements, are basically alike in their parabolic form and function. We conclude therefore that Isa. 5:1-7 is best understood as a juridical parable.

3. Delineation of Wisdom Features

Most commentators are agreed that Isaiah probably recited his parable of judgment at a vintage festival, possibly the Feast of Tabernacles (Deut. 16:13-15; Exod. 23:16; 34:22; Lev. 23:34-43). Such festivals were joyous occasions in the life of

---

[55] Cf. Westermann, p. 145: "In dem Gleichnis Jes. 5, 1-7 ist unter der Einkleidung das GV [i.e., Gerichtsankündigung gegen Israel] in allen Teilen zu erkennen."

[56] This is U. Simon's characterization; see U. Simon, "The Poor Man's Ewe-Lamb. An Example of a Juridical Parable," *Biblica* 48 (1967): 207-42, esp. 208.

[57] Cf. Simon's analysis (*ibid.*).

the community, where it was appropriate to sing popular ballads. Hence Isaiah assumes the posture of the ballad singer. From the content of the song, Isaiah more specifically stands as the "friend of the bridegroom," who seems to have a function comparable to our best man.[58] Again, it is clear that one of Isaiah's primary intentions for adopting the role of a singer and for using a parable was to force Israel into pronouncing self-judgment and hence to acknowledge the rightness of divine judgment.

That Isaiah chooses a parabolic form, a didactic device, is the significant thing for our purpose. Why does he opt for a wisdom form and technique? To answer this question one must analyze more carefully the affinities between Isaiah's approach and the wise man's. First of all, like the wise man, Isaiah draws an incident from the experience of man and nature in order to get across a forceful and foreboding message to his hearers. It is important to point out that for the ancients the parable would have more than merely illustrative import. As we noted in our exegesis of the parable in Isa. 1:3, a basic affinity exists between the "natural" and the human spheres: an experience from the former could have "a relationship of correspondence" to one in the latter.[59] For instance, we read in Hebrew Wisdom Literature:

> Like clouds and wind without rain
> is a man who boasts of a gift he does not give
> (Prov. 25:14).

> Like a dog that returns to his vomit
> is a fool that repeats his folly (Prov. 26:11).

> He [i.e. the righteous man] is like a tree
> planted by streams of water,
> that yields its fruit in its season,
> and its leaf does not wither.
> In all that he does he prospers.
> The wicked are not so,
> but are like the chaff which the wind drives away
> (Ps. 1:3-4).

[58] Junker, p. 264.
[59] G. von Rad, *Old Testament Theology* I: 424.

> Do not praise a man for his good looks,
> nor loathe a man because of his appearance.
> The bee is small among flying creatures,
> but her product is the best of sweet things
> (Sir. 11:2-3) .

> Like flourishing leaves on a spreading tree
> which sheds some and puts forth others,
> so are the generations of flesh and blood:
> one dies and another is born (Sir. 14:19) .

> The fruit discloses the cultivation
> of a tree;
> so the expression of a thought
> discloses the cultivation of a man's mind (Sir. 27:6) .

"These examples . . . state analogies," says von Rad, "between processes of 'nature' and the life of man. Thus the point of these maxims is a comparison of totally different realms of order, which yet reveal analogous phenomena and which can therefore be co-ordinated." [60] The same sort of procedure seems to be at work in Isaiah's parable, though the analogy is more complex than the illustrations cited above. On the one hand, the vineyard (=loved one) that produces worthless grapes becomes an analogy of Israel's failure to produce "righteousness" and "justice"; on the other, the owner's (=the lover) announcement of destruction becomes the analogy of Yahweh's sentence of doom for Israel. In any case, there is a correspondence between the two sets of phenomena, which otherwise lie on different planes. The dialectic within the analogy between the owner's "action" (=Yahweh's love for Israel) and the vineyard's "reaction" (=Israel's sin) is most striking: careful toil reaped a bitter harvest. This was just the opposite of what was expected according to the laws of both the natural and the divine-human spheres. This "surprise element" is often found in parables.[61] The opening lines of the love song would lead one to expect a happy ending. But such is not the case, for the parable takes an unexpected turn. Something from every-

[60] *Ibid.*, p. 425.
[61] R. W. Funk, *Language, Hermeneutic, and Word of God* (New York: Harper & Row, 1966) , pp. 160-61.

day life—the love of a man for a woman—is given a cruel twist, for love's labor was lost on a blatant ingrate. Hence like the wise man, Isaiah shows a penchant for appealing to the basic order of the world and experience. He uses the unnatural turn of events to give greater grounds for divine judgment. Also, Isaiah's demand of a decision from the listeners is a tremendous technique, for they unwittingly pronounce their own judgment and so justify the correctness of the divine verdict of judgment. That they had agreed to the owner's verdict of judgment against the vineyard forces them to acknowledge the validity of Yahweh's verdict of judgment. In light of criteria drawn both from general experience and from legal precedent, their action was reprehensible and the judgment was justified.

When one steps back and looks at the whole poem, he sees a rhetorically and poetically gifted individual at work. First of all, to distract the attention of his audience from his real intent, Isaiah adopts the role of the ballad singer. Moreover, he draws away their attention still further by moving immediately into the realm of metaphor—the vineyard is a maiden and the owner is her lover. The audience is captivated by an age-old and perennial human theme—the tragedy of betrayed love. That Isaiah calls on them to give judgment is very understandable psychologically, for they, like all such observers of broken love affairs, are all too happy to give quick judgment. Isaiah's resonance with the emotions of his listeners is striking. Finally, he turns the tables on his audience, equating them with the vineyard and summarizing Yahweh's indictment. Isaiah then lets the audience draw the implications of the prior sentence of doom which they unwittingly thought was just punishment for the unfaithful maiden in the love song. The sudden transition from the imaginary world of love poetry to the real world of eighth-century Judah forced the listeners to come to grips with their own desperate situation. The impact must have been shattering as the realization of the prophet's true intention dawned. The irony of the whole situation is painfully clear. All in all Isaiah unveils a profound technique, utilizing multiple stages of metaphoric logic, combining adroitly imagery and terminology from the diverse realms of nature and law, and irresistibly drawing his audience into an ironic participation in the drama of a tragic love affair. That Isaiah emerges here as a poet and preacher of rare powers goes without saying.

The comparison of Isa. 5:1-7 with the parable in 1:3 is instructive. Both talk of Yahweh's disappointment with Israel in terms of a long history of apostasy; both employ a wisdom tack in appealing to world order to emphasize the unnatural quality of Israel's apostasy; both correlate two sets of phenomena from different realms, discerning a certain correspondence; both, in short, use a pedagogical technique. To be sure, there is also a definite contrast between the two parables. Isa. 5:1-7 has a much more complex symbolic structure with its double metaphor of Vineyard=Loved one=Israel and of Owner=Lover=Yahweh. Also, in Isa. 5 the prophet goes beyond mere indictment to the actual sentence of doom. The important thing for our purpose, however, is that they are similar in utilizing a wisdom tack.

C. THE PARABLE OF THE FARMER (ISA. 28:23-29)

While clothed in simple garb, the well-known parable of the farmer has long challenged interpreters in quest of the enigmatic implications of its meaning. Though a few scholars[62] have called it non-Isaianic, the vast majority do not question its Isaianic vintage. Since the speech is loaded with wisdom features, it is fundamental in the assessment of Isaiah's relationship to the wisdom tradition. Hence it demands careful and complete examination.

The text is cryptic at a few places, but fortunately not in a way that would cripple an interpretative effort.

---

[62] E.g., T. K. Cheyne, *Introduction to the Book of Isaiah* (London: Adam and Charles Clark, 1895), pp. 184 ff.; G. Boström, *Proverbiastudien* (Lund: G. W. K. Gleerup, 1928), pp. 69-70; R. H. Pfeiffer, *Introduction to the Old Testament* (New York: Harper & Bros., 1948), p. 420. It is interesting to note in passing the bias of Cheyne in his rejection of the passage, for it reveals something of the basic attitude of a whole generation of scholarship toward the relationship of prophets and wisdom: "It is not likely that Isaiah (who was heart and soul a prophet) imitated proverbial writers" (p. 186).

Give ear, and hear my voice;
give heed and hear my speech.

Does he who plows for sowing plow continually,
and [continually] open and harrow his soil?
Does he not, after he has leveled its surface,
scatter dill, sow cummin,
put in wheat in rows (שורה)
barley in a correct place (נסמן) [63]
and spelt at its edges?

And he is instructed correctly,
his God teaches him.

For dill is not threshed with a sledge,
nor is a cart wheel rolled over cummin,
but dill is beaten out with a stick
and cummin with a staff.

Does one crush bread grain?
No, he surely does not thresh it forever.[64]
When he drives his cart wheel over it,
with his horses he does not crush it.

This also comes from Yahweh of hosts;
He is wonderful in counsel
and great in wisdom.

[63] In spite of the difficulties of שורה and נסמן, the RSV makes as good sense as can be had, though of course certainty cannot be attained. Some commentators (B. Duhm, *Das Buch Jesaia* [Göttingen: Vandenhoeck & Ruprecht, 1902], p. 174; *et al.*) have eliminated the two words as corrupt dittographs of the following ושערה and וכסמת respectively. Although the LXX omits both words, it is too corrupt in this passage to be used as a trustworthy criterion. Happily, the sense is not appreciably altered whether one leaves them out or stays with the MT. S. C. Thexton, while retaining the words, has given an alternative reading that smacks more of unwarranted speculation than solid textual work (see his article, "A Note on Isaiah XXVIII, 25 and 28," VT 2 [1952]: 81-82).

[64] S. C. Thexton (pp. 81-82) sets forth an interesting alternative to the usual understanding of this line. First, he takes the לחם יודק as a statement, rejecting the view that reads it as a question. Secondly, to mitigate the apparent contradiction in the לא ידוקנו at the end of the verse, he reads the לא absolutely ("no"). Thus his translation runs: "Corn for bread has to be ground. For he does not go on threshing it indefinitely—clattering his wagon wheels (over it) and winnowing it; —no—he has to crush it." The fatal flaw of this translation is his reading of the לא: to sever the לא from the following imperfect and understand

1. Preliminary Analysis of Structure and Style

Easily marked off from the preceding and following units, the passage has formal and content breaks at both ends. The call to attention formula in vs. 23 signals a fresh beginning which is confirmed by the sharp change in tone and content in the following description of the purposefulness and divine origin of the farmer's activities. A completely new oracle begins in 29:1 ff., with a different form (a "woe" oracle) and theme (announcement of doom for Jerusalem). We have, then, in Isa. 28:23-29 a well-defined, complete speech unit.

Characterized by deft balance the passage displays striking symmetry in its structure. Isaiah leads off with a typical call to attention (vs. 23). Next comes a wise man's teaching on the nature and origin of the farmer's skills (vss. 24-28). A concluding generalization nicely rounds off the unit (vs. 29). An outline puts the matter clearly:

  I. A call to attention (vs. 23)

  II. Questions demonstrating the farmer's skills (plowing and sowing (vss. 24-25)

    A. Question evoking a *negative* answer (vs. 24)

    B. Question evoking a *positive* answer (vs. 25)

  III. The reason for his skills—their divine origin (vs. 26)

  IV. Further demonstration of the farmer's skills (threshing and crushing grains) (vss. 27-28)

    A. A statement about threshing techniques (vs. 27)

    B. A question and answer about techniques of crushing grain (vs. 28)

  V. A summary-appraisal (vs. 29)

    A. The summary: The reason for the farmer's skills— their divine origin (vs. 29*a*)

    B. The appraisal: The wonderful quality of Yahweh's counsel and wisdom (vs. 29*b*)

As unanimously agreed, the passage is closely patterned

---

the former in an absolute sense defies the rules of Hebrew grammar and is highly tenuous. His so-called corroborative examples of the absolute use of לא (Gen. 19:2; Job 23:6) have a different syntactical pattern and simply cannot be used as parallels. Hence his translation is to be rejected.

along the lines of a wisdom teaching or *mashal*.[65] From every angle the evidence is conclusive: content, speech forms, and general didactic tone betray the solid wisdom roots. Technical wisdom language abounds.[66] The chief topic—that the farmer's skills stem from a divine teacher—is wisdom in orientation (vss. 26, 29). Moreover, individual speech forms common to wisdom are plentiful. The lead-off formula, called aptly a *"Lehröffnungsformel"* by H. W. Wolff,[67] occurs frequently in wisdom literature to introduce a lesson (e.g., Prov. 4:1; 7:24; Job 33:1, 31; 34:2; Ps. 49:2; *et al.*)[68] The didactic questions (vss. 27, 28b)—all containing truths gained by empirical observation—bear the imprint of wisdom's hand.[69] Finally, the concluding verse has the markings of a sage's reflection and its terminology is securely grounded in wisdom; in fact, B. S. Childs[70] has identified it as a distinctive wisdom form, naming it the "Summary-Appraisal."

Further confirmation of the dominant wisdom perspective is found in the international character of the passage's teach-

[65] On *mashal*, see the still basic study of O. Eissfeldt, *Der Maschal im Alten Testament.*

[66] E.g., יסר and ירה (vs. 26); עצה and תושיה (vs. 29). Of the ninety-four times the root ירה appears in the Old Testament, forty-two are in Proverbs and Job. (For a complete classification and study of this root, see J. A. Sanders, *Suffering as Divine Discipline in the Old Testament and Post-Biblical Judaism* (Rochester: Colgate Rochester Divinity School Bulletin XXVIII [1955].) ירי of course has roots in priestly circles as well as in wisdom (cf. the study of G. Östborn, *Torah in the Old Testament* [Lund: Haakon Ohlsson, 1945], pp. 112 ff.). For the wisdom background of עצה, see below Chapter IV, "Counsel/Counsellor and Jerusalem Court Wisdom"; also P. A. H. de Boer, "The Counsellor," VTS 3 (1955): 150-61. תושיה does not occur nearly so frequently as the above terms; it is completely in the ambience of wisdom (cf. Prov. 2:7; 3:21; 8:14; 18:1; Job 5:12; 6:13; 11:6; 12:16; 26:3; see also Mic. 6:9 where it is problematic).

[67] Wolff, *Hosea*, p. 123. A literal English rendition is somewhat wooden: "Formula for the Opening of Instruction." I question Wolff's conclusion that this was *originally* and exclusively a wisdom formula which was then picked up by other circles.

[68] Cf. also the opening of the Teaching of Amenemope (ANET, p. 421).

[69] This type of empirical observation constituted much of the wise men's activity (cf. the fine discussion of von Rad, *Old Testament Theology* I: 418 ff.).

[70] Childs, *Isaiah and the Assyrian Crisis*, pp. 128 ff.

ing. Like many other Old Testament wisdom texts, it has relatives in the ancient world. In fact, the view that the farmer ultimately owes his agricultural skills to his God who is the wisdom teacher par excellence (vss. 26, 29a) seems to be a widespread phenomenon. An old Sumerian ancestor can be found in the so-called "Farmer's Almanac" (*ca.* 1780 B.C.), which ends on the note that agricultural rules come from the god Ninurta.[71] Likewise, Vergil's *Georgics* contains a poem on the farmer's activities that speaks of the deity as the instructor of peasants (1. 35 ff.). In neither of these cases is there a question of direct linkage with the Isaianic passage, nor anything more than a general similarity in form; they only exemplify the ancients' propensity to put everything under a divine umbrella. Independent outgrowths of similar approaches to reality, they highlight well the international flavor and the religious orientation of ancient wisdom.

To summarize: Isa. 28:23-29 is an independent speech, marked by a beautifully balanced structure. It swarms with wisdom characteristics and can be set in the context of ancient Near Eastern wisdom.

2. Basic Problems of Interpretation

Once the bare description of structure, style, and wisdom features has been given, the fundamental problems of interpretation begin to emerge. That the prophet is using wisdom teaching to stress the purposefulness and divine source of the farmer's technique is obvious. But where does one go from here? Why is such a passage used in the present context? What purpose does it serve? The only thing clear is that the meaning and function of the speech in its Isaianic context demand more exact explication.

[71] S. N. Kramer, *History Begins at Sumer* (London: Thames and Hudson, 1958), pp. 105 ff., esp. 108. In an earlier publication (*Sumerian Literary Texts from Nippur: The Annual of the American Schools of Oriental Research,* Vol. XXIII for 1943-44 [New Haven, 1944]: 36), he gives a translation of the appropriate part: "The Instructions of Ninurta, the son of Enlil; Ninurta, steadfast farmer of Enlil, good is thy praise." (I owe this parallel to H. Cazelles, "Les Débuts de la Sagesse en Israël," *Les sagesses du Proche-Orient ancien,* p. 32.)

1. It must be admitted at the outset that many obstacles stand in the way of arriving at a satisfactory interpretation. First, the larger context of chap. 28 is treacherously complex.[72] It has long been recognized that the chapter is a collection of speeches, given over a wide span of time to a variety of audiences, but now welded into a thematic unity. For instance, the proud drunkards of Samaria (28:1 ff.), who were swept away by a flood of divine wrath, become a paradigm of judgment for the equally arrogant scoffers of Judah and Jerusalem (28: 7 ff.). The heterogeneous makeup of the chapter, however, renders its usefulness as a contextual court of appeal a tricky and potentially tenuous affair. One cannot therefore leap to the conclusion that the present speech is an intrinsic and original part of the preceding context and read everything on the same flat plane; he must rather be alert to the different levels on which the connections have been made.

Secondly, the speech is bereft of an explicit identification of the addressees. In contrast to other Isaianic speeches that have a call to attention formula,[73] the audience here is not named or more narrowly defined; in fact, we have only the vague plural address in the opening string of imperatives. The reference in the preceding unit to "priest" and "prophet" (vs. 7) or to "scoffers" (vs. 14; cf. vs. 22) cannot be automatically read in, since, as just indicated, the two units have an original independence and do not necessarily involve the same audience. It is theoretically possible that the speech could have been spoken to a general audience of Israelites, to the prophet's disciples, or to a group of hostile critics.[74] As we shall attempt to show, however, there are internal criteria that tip the balance in favor of the last alternative—at least in the original stage of the tradition.

Finally, the speech lacks a direct application. Hence the ex-

[72] Cf. the basic analysis of Duhm, pp. 165 ff.

[73] Cf. Isa. 1:2, 10; 28:14; 32:9.

[74] Most commentators opt for the last alternative, but others (e.g., O. Procksch, *Jesaia* I, KAT IX [Leipzig: D. Werner Scholl, 1930]: 368; and J. Fischer, *Das Buch Isaias I* [Bonn: Peter Hanstein, 1937]: 191) understand the addressees as the prophet's disciples. Still others (e.g., Smith, p. 165) see the addressees more broadly as Israelites in general.

act point that the prophet wants to get across is left somewhat in the air. For some[75] this has been sufficient warrant to hang a non-Isaianic label on the speech, but this is a tenuous judgment since parables often lack a direct application.[76] However judged, it should surely put the brakes to any overconfident interpretation that veers wildly into the realm of uncontrolled speculation.

2. Though now alerted to some of the formidable difficulties, we are still left with the problem of defining more precisely the speech's form and function in its Isaianic context. Scholars have offered different options for consideration: (a) Should it be taken at face value and be read simply as a wise man's teaching on the nature and origin of agricultural practices?[77] (b) Is it an allegory, depicting in the farmer's multiple activities the details of Yahweh's program in history?[78] (c) Or, as most interpreters think, is it some type of parable?[79] If so, can the function and intention of the parable be more precisely defined? What is the existential and historical situation in which it was used?

To see the speech merely as a wise man's teaching on farming is not likely for a number of reasons. First, the speaker seems to be arguing for a point that goes beyond an affirmation concerning the nature of the farmer's skills,[80] for this would already command assent. Why argue for what is already agreed upon? Secondly, thematic links exist between the speech and the mainstream of Isaiah's message—to name the most outstanding, the "counsel" (עֵצָה) of Yahweh.[81] These links point

[75] E.g., Boström, pp. 69-70.
[76] Cf. Bultmann, pp. 182 ff.; Jeremias, p. 105; Funk, pp. 134 ff.
[77] Boström, pp. 69-70.
[78] E.g., Cheyne, pp. 184-85. Both F. Delitzsch and R. B. Y. Scott call it a parable, but attempt to draw out allegorical nuances (for the former, see his *Biblical Commentary on the Prophecies of Isaiah*, trans. James Martin [Grand Rapids: Wm. B. Eerdmans, 1957], p. 16; for the latter, see *The Book of Isaiah*, Vol. VI in *The Interpreter's Bible* [Nashville: Abingdon Press, 1956]: 321.
[79] So the great majority of the standard commentaries.
[80] The disputational character of the speech will be discussed below.
[81] This point has also been made by L. J. Liebreich, "The Parable Taken from the Farmer's Labors in Is. XXVIII, 23-29" (Hebr.) *Tarbiz* XXIV/2 (1955) : 126-28. (See the English summary in the *Internationale*

to a specialized usage in the Isaianic context. Lastly, the very presence of the speech in a distinctly prophetic context would lead one to suspect that a special purpose was being served beyond a wise man's interest in agronomy.[82] Reading the speech on a flat level ignores these factors. Hence we would conclude that the speech is more than a sage's lesson.

Allegory of any breed has little to commend it as a satisfying approach. It is vitiated by the notable absence of any explicit clues which would clearly indicate that the different facets of the farmer's labors are to be understood as allegorical symbols of God's program in history. In light of this absence, it is most in keeping with the data to lay aside the allegorical approach as improbable.

The parabolic interpretation, in spite of the difficulties, still has the most weight on its side. It satisfies, on the one hand, the intrinsic demand of the speech to have a significance larger than that of a simple wisdom teaching. On the other hand, it sidesteps the snare of an allegorical exegesis by avoiding the fruitless quest for hidden meanings and by seeking rather the fundamental thrust of the comparison. Therefore, as often happens in wisdom, an activity from the realm of everyday experiences becomes an analogy for another truth.[83]

3. Although the parabolic nature of the speech has long been noted, sharper clarity only began to emerge when the parable's disputational character was recognized. B. Duhm was one of the first to perceive its argumentative character: "The *mashal* is an answer to the previously mentioned scoffing at his prophecies. . . . It defends the prophet against the scornful reproach that his threats have not been fulfilled." [84] Thus the *mashal* was a self-vindication of the prophet. Duhm came to

---

Zeitschriftenschau für Bibelwissenschaft und Grenzgebiete, Band IV, Heft 1-2 [Düsseldorf: Patmos Verlag, 1955/56].) See further Chapter IV, "Counsel/Counsellor and Jerusalem Court Wisdom."

[82] Even if one were to follow the view that the speech is non-Isaianic and was added much later by a wise man, he would still have to explain its function in the present context.

[83] For a discussion of this propensity of the wise, cf. von Rad, *Old Testament Theology* I: 424 ff., and Gese, p. 35.

[84] Duhm, p. 175.

his interpretation largely on the basis of contextual considerations: since the prophet added no application, one must discern the meaning of the speech from the larger context. Though this tack has a degree of validity, it is not completely convincing because it is not grounded more firmly on specific evidence from the text. As observed above, the context alone is shaky grounds for an interpretation. Also, as we shall attempt to show, Duhm's interpretation of the point under dispute—the defense of the prophetic message—is not completely correct. Duhm, then, while on the right track, stopped short of a cogent interpretation. He failed to see the speech's internal affinities with the disputation and did not perceive clearly the real issue under debate.

It fell to the form critics to demonstrate more convincingly the disputational nature of the parable. J. Begrich,[85] following the lead of Gunkel, made the basic analysis of disputation speech. It arose from the pattern of disagreement within the community. Involving such speech forms as question and answer, assertion and counterassertion, it seeks to convince an opponent and win him over to your position. That the prophets reflect disputation speech is clear.[86] Often following a collision course vis-à-vis public opinion, they inevitably found themselves in situations of conflict. Therefore they adopted the "disputation," says Begrich, "because they saw themselves placed repeatedly before the necessity to deal with objections in order to defend their viewpoint and to convince their opponents." [87] In assuming the stance of a disputant, the prophets changed their usual posture as a commissioned messenger of Yahweh's Word, for in a sense they stood on the same level as their opponents in order to meet head on any objections to their message.[88] This change in Isaiah's under-

---

[85] Begrich, *Studien zu Deuterojesaja*, pp. 48 ff. Cf. also Westermann, pp. 144-45; *idem*, "Sprache und Struktur der Prophetie Deuterojesajas," *Forschung am Alten Testament* ("Theologische Bücherei," 24; München: Chr. Kaiser, 1964), pp. 124 ff.

[86] Amos 3:3 ff.; 9:7; Isa. 10:8-11; Jer. 2; 8:1; Mal.; *et al.*

[87] Begrich, p. 49.

[88] Westermann stresses this change in prophetic posture (*Grundformen prophetischer Rede*, pp. 144 ff.; *Forschung am Alten Testament*, p. 125).

standing of his role is expressed in the opening call to attention, where he explicitly labels what he is going to say as "my voice"//"my speech" (vs. 23).

Now we must look more closely at the inner development of the speech in order to discern its character as a disputation as well as the function it serves. Isaiah carefully constructs a basis of agreement, using the common knowledge of the nature and origin of the farmer's activity (see again the structural analysis). None of his hearers would dispute the obvious—that the farmer follows a purposeful pattern in his various activities and that his knowledge derives ultimately from God. The basic point is that the farmer does different things at different times and in different ways—and all with a rationale that is divine in origin. Following the introductory call to attention come two rhetorical questions relating to the orderly phases in farming: the first question elicits a negative response (vs. 24), the second an affirmative (vs. 25). Such rhetorical questions, which draw their material from everyday experience, are frequently found in disputation speech and especially show a kinship to wisdom teaching.[89] Common knowledge is appealed to in order to evoke assent and to give a basis for argument. Part IV (vss. 27-28) stands as a counterpart to Part II (vss. 24-25) and rounds out the picture of the farmer's activities. Together they simply constitute parts of the whole and are not to be construed as serving different functions or having different meanings. In both II and IV the farmer's sense of timing is interwoven with his different practices; taken together they underscore forcefully the same point. In Part IV (vss. 27-28) Isaiah uses simple statements plus a question and answer scheme (vs. 28) to describe the techniques involved in threshing and crushing different kinds of grain. Both II and IV are followed with an assertion that the farmer owes his knowledge to divine instruction (vss. 26, 29a), which gives the motivation

[89] E.g., the duplex type of rhetorical question is a favorite one (cf. Amos 6:12; Jer. 12:5; Prov. 6:27; Job 6:5-6; 8:11; et al.). For didactic questions used in a clearly disputational setting, cf. Amos 3:3-6, 8; Ps. 94:8 ff.; Isa. 40:21 ff.; see also Wolff's discussion of the didactic question form in terms of its disputational function and wisdom roots (Amos' geistige Heimat, pp. 5 ff.).

or rationale of his agricultural skills. Again, this would command immediate and unquestioned assent in the ancient world.

On the basis of the agreement elicited from the hearers concerning the nature and source of the farmer's activities, Isaiah then concludes with a generalization: Yahweh is "wonderful in counsel, and excellent in wisdom" (vs. 29*b*). This climactic affirmation is the best clue we have as to the essential point at stake in the dispute. It would seem that Isaiah employs the activity of the divinely taught farmer as one manifestation of the structure of reality suspended under the canopy of divine wisdom. Or, to change the metaphor, the farmer's wise activity is a mirror that reflects the more brilliant light of its divine source. So Isaiah's argument seems to run as follows: if the unpretentious farmer works with such skill and design, then how much greater must God so work, since he is the source of the farmer's knowledge.[90] Like the farmer, Yahweh

[90] Many commentators have recognized the implicit *a fortiori* argument; they have not, however, given full heed to it and have concentrated on the farmer as a parabolic (or allegorical) representation of God. Now to be sure, an analogy between the farmer and God is involved in the argument. Too often, however, this analogy has been misconstrued. By failing to see fully the function the farmer's portrait plays in the argument (i.e., to establish a basis of argeement), the majority of interpreters have erred in trying to read the details of the farmer's work as symbols of God's activity in history. In so doing, they have repeated the mistake of many exegetes of the disputation speech in Amos 3:3–6:8, who tried to interpret the didactic questions in terms of the symbolic truth they allegedly contained. Recent scholarship has corrected this mistaken approach and has demonstrated that Amos only used the series of questions as analogies in his argument in order to show the logic of his conclusion (3:8).

Recently G. Fohrer (*Das Buch Jesaia* II ["Zürcher Bibelkommentare"; Zürich-Stuttgart: Zwingli Verlag, 1962]: 66-67) has offered an alternative to the view that posits an analogy between the farmer and God. Although he agrees that the parable functions as a disputation speech, he criticizes the consensus on the interpretation of the analogy. Since God is named alongside the farmer, it is incongruous, he argues, that the latter could be a symbolic representation of God. The farmer is better understood as analogous to Isaiah—another divinely taught person. The main difficulty with this position is that the speech fails to give any explicit indication that the farmer is analogous to the prophet; otherwise it is a good theory. Fohrer's observation that the farmer is named alongside God does not really militate against seeing an analogy between the two; for to have

does different things at different times. In assenting to the evidence of divine wisdom visible in the farmer's labors, the hearers must agree with the cogency of the prophet's affirmation concerning the impeccable quality of Yahweh's wisdom and counsel. Yahweh's actions, like the farmer's, bear one of the hallmarks of wisdom—namely, the ability to match the proper method with the proper time. Thus the central point of the parable as well as the issue at stake in the dispute is found in the basic structure of the agreement and comes out most clearly in the concluding claim about the nature of Yahweh's wisdom. That Yahweh's wisdom was a point of contention in Isaiah's confrontation with the people is attested by his oracles. In fact, the clash of opinion over "counsel" and "wisdom" fills many scenes in Isaiah's prophetic activity.[91] He proclaims the terms of Yahweh's wise counsel [92] (14:24-27; 31:2a), while simultaneously pronouncing a dour diatribe against the foolish, ineffectual counsel of Israel or the nations (5:21; 7:5, 7; 29:15; 30:1). Conversely, that the people and especially the leaders were critical of Yahweh's counsel is also evidenced. A lineup of key oracles will illustrate the nature of the conflict:

(1) Isaiah's condemnation of Israel's wisdom and counsel:

> Woe to those who are wise in their own eyes,
>   and shrewd in their own sight! (5:21)

> Woe to those who hide deep from Yahweh their counsel.
>   (29:15a)

> Therefore, behold, I will again
>   do marvelous things with this people,
>   wonderful and marvelous;
> and the wisdom of their wise men shall perish,
>   and the discernment of their discerning men shall
>   be hid. (29:14)

> Woe to the rebellious children who carry out a counsel
>   but not mine. (30:1)

---

both side by side in a teacher-student relationship is intrinsic to the essential structure of the argument.

[91] This has also been emphasized by Liebreich, pp. 126-28.

[92] The subject of Yahweh's "Counsel" requires a separate examination, so important is it to Isaiah's message (see Chapter IV).

(2) The people's criticism of Yahweh's wisdom:

Let him make haste, let him speed his work that we may
   see it;
Let the counsel of the Holy One of Israel draw near,
   and let it come, that we may know it! (5:19)

(3) Isaiah's claim concerning Yahweh's wisdom:

He is wonderful in counsel,
   and great in wisdom. (28:29*b*) .

Against this kind of background it seems appropriate to interpret the parable and its claim about Yahweh's counsel and wisdom. Isaiah argues that Yahweh's activities always followed
a purposeful pattern and that it is wrong for Israel's leaders
to contend that Yahweh was haphazard in his action. To Isaiah
there was a consistent and wise purpose in Yahweh's actions,
even though that purpose might be hidden and seem haphazard in the ambiguities of history. Here is a beautiful illustration of how Isaiah appropriated wisdom tradition as one
way to wrestle with the problem of Yahweh's activity in history. To G. von Rad, in fact, the parable furnishes "written
evidence of [Isaiah's] expressly rational grappling with history." [93] Isaiah, arguing like a wise man, saw a fundamental
affinity between agricultural activities and historical events:
both bore the stamp of Yahweh's wisdom and counsel. This
manifestation of Yahweh's wisdom in these two apparently
disparate spheres shows the fallacy of separating too rigidly between "nature" and history in the Old Testament; for Isaiah
at least it was the same God who effected his wise counsel in
both spheres.

If it is correct that the basic intention of the parable is to
defend the wisdom of Yahweh's action in history, it is now
pertinent to ask whether the dimensions of his action can be
more exactly defined from the content of the parable. As we
have already indicated, the parable lacks a clear-cut application. It is possible, however, to reconstruct with some degree

[93] G. von Rad, *Old Testament Theology* II, trans. D. M. G. Stalker
(New York: Harper & Row, 1965) : 184.

of probability a concrete setting for the parable which would give more insight into its specific intention. If the interpretation of the parable as disputation is correct and if the most likely historical situation was that of the Assyrian crisis in 701 B.C., then it is possible that the parable serves as Isaiah's answer to the questions of Judah's despondent leaders and populace following the devastation of the Assyrian invasion. If this be the case, the parable's intent would go beyond the more formal argument over the efficacy of Yahweh's wisdom and would center on the intensely real issue of the nature of Yahweh's plans for Judah as she faced a dark and foreboding future. Here the burning question concerned the possibility that Yahweh had forsaken his people and would continue to leave them exposed to foreign invaders. What did the future hold? Would Yahweh punish forever or would he relent?

Older commentators too easily interpreted the parable as a clear-cut promise of salvation. Here the interpretation moved into an allegory of sorts in which such words as "harrowing," "plowing," "beating-out," "threshing," and "crushing" symbolized the present devastations perpetrated by the Assyrian army. According to this interpretation, the precise intention of the parable is to announce that just as the farmer does not continually break up the soil, so Yahweh will not judge forever.[94] On the contrary, Yahweh will alter his activity in the future and save Judah. So the parable finally comes out as a promise of salvation and a message of comfort.

The difficulty with such an interpretation is that it rationalizes elements in the parable into clear-cut categories of judgment and salvation when the parable itself does not admit such rationalization.[95] As we have seen, the description of the orderly phases of the farmer's activities is given in order to

[94] Cf. Smith, pp. 165-66: "If the husbandman be so methodical and careful, shall the God who taught him not also be? If the violent treatment of the lands and fruits be so measured and adapted for their greater fruitfulness and purity, ought we not to trust God to have the same intentions in his violent treatment of his people?" Cf. also Delitzsch, *Isaiah*, II: 16; F. Fischer, p. 192.

[95] Cf. Funk, pp. 151 ff., for an illuminating treatment of the nature of parabolic language.

demonstrate the thesis that Yahweh, like the farmer, acts wisely even though he does different things at different times. To move from here into an allegory of Yahweh's acts of judgment and salvation would seem therefore to be an unwarranted and erroneous step. Moreover, it limits the parable's meaning by giving it a specific application. The main point is that the orderly phases reflect and illustrate the wisdom of the divine source and thus by analogy point to the fact that Yahweh always acts wisely. Finally, this interpretation perceives a certainty in the prophet's words which the prophet himself seems to lack. One recalls that Isaiah does not speak here with the customary prophetic certainty; there is no explicit appeal to divine authority, for the parable lacks a "Thus says Yahweh." In fact, as we have noted, the prophet makes a point of saying expressly that it is *his* words (vs. 23). Hence the style and substance of the prophet's speech would seem to have a different intent from giving an unequivocal promise (contrast the promissory element in Isa. 28:16, 17*a*).

It is more in keeping, therefore, with the basic open-endedness of the parable to reject the interpretation that it contains a clear-cut promise of salvation for the future. In contrast I suggest that the parable is better read as Isaiah's way of addressing a despondent, distraught Judah in a time of uncertainty and clouded vision—his own as well as Judah's.[96] Isaiah is giving his reflections and arguments on the present crisis of faith, utilizing the wise man's approach to the future which was based not on a vision but on an assessment of the future in terms of analogy. He is arguing that Yahweh, like the wise farmer, will not continue to do the same thing. Thus, if the analogy is sound, Yahweh will not continue to punish; the shattering devastations will cease. But the argument lacks the certainty of a vision vouchsafed from Yahweh. Isaiah seems to be saying, "I have no special message from Yahweh; so I cannot give a special word of promise. Yet I can give you my reflections as to the probable course of Yahweh's future actions. Since we may count on God being as wise as the farmer, we

[96] For what follows I am indebted to Professor Rolf Knierim for some stimulating suggestions given in an informal discussion.

may trust that he will not punish forever." Hence Isaiah is arguing that in the midst of a dark present and a clouded, threatening future, one is still called upon to trust Yahweh to act wisely.

Such an interpretation would comport well with the emphasis in Isaiah's other oracles where Isaiah continually calls upon leaders and people alike to keep faith in Yahweh (cf. Isa. 7:4, 9; 28:12a, 16b). Also it is noteworthy that in another period of crisis Isaiah says he will withdraw in the face of rejection, but that he will continue to hope in Yahweh (Isa. 8:16 ff.). In the crisis of 701 B.C., Isaiah affirms the need to retain trust in Yahweh and argues that there is a basis for hope, but also indicates that he has no clear word from Yahweh. What he can give is a prognosis of hope; he can answer the cries of skepticism and despair by reflecting on the quality of Yahweh's wisdom from the analogy of the farmer. To be sure, he is conceding the dark ambiguities of Yahweh's present activities. He can only deal with the future in light of the present à la the wise man and argue that Yahweh will not act foolishly and capriciously and so will not likely punish Judah forever.

In conclusion one can say initially that the parable is best not construed as an unequivocal promise of salvation. It is rather to be interpreted as an argument for a beneficent purpose in Yahweh's future activity, even though there is no room for joyous optimism. Isaiah attempts to convince despondent critics that if one grants wisdom to God, then one can trust Yahweh to act as the farmer and not continue to punish Judah. In the context of disputation, the parable is both a prognosis for the future and a call for decision—that is, Isaiah forces his skeptical opponents to decide whether or not Yahweh is a God who can be counted on to act wisely and hence can be trusted. Isaiah is calling on his opponents to recognize that Yahweh's actions can be depended upon to be ultimately wise and beneficent in the future despite the ambiguities of the present hour. He is saying that Yahweh's wisdom is as transparently clear as the farmer's, if one only looks and takes note. It would be only a fool who could miss the wisdom of the farmer's actions and so only a fool who could miss the wisdom of Yahweh's actions. If this parable was given in the context of the Assyrian crisis in 701 B.C., it is indeed a probing and challenging argument—an argument which calls for involvement, forces a decision, and holds out the hope of a brighter future.

3. Text and Tradition

We must now assess the importance of the parable for our general problem of Isaiah's relationship to wisdom traditions. In this regard the parable is especially significant because of its frontline role in demonstrating the influence of wisdom on Isaiah. Coming at a crucial spot—the defense of the wisdom of Yahweh's activities—it highlights well the way Isaiah appropriated wisdom teaching and turned it to his own purpose. Here the parable is not an illustrative appendage, but instead constitutes the essential structure and substance of Isaiah's argument.

One cannot be content with this general statement, however, for he must go on and ask for the possible motives or reasons behind Isaiah's usage of a distinctively wisdom speech to defend Yahweh's wisdom. First of all, one can say that the parable was appropriate for the disputational setting which demands a line of argumentation where one appeals to evidence that would immediately command assent. So one of the constituent elements of wisdom—the appeal to empirical data—is eminently suitable for disputation. In this sense the wisdom form is very apropos. However, this is surely not the only factor, for there are other speech genres that can be used in disputes.

A second motive may lie in the nature of the subject matter under dispute—the wisdom of Yahweh's actions in history. It is understandable why Isaiah would opt for a wisdom form to deal with the problem of Yahweh's wisdom. By using a parable Isaiah is able to argue on the same ground as his opponents. In such a context, his utilization of wisdom materials is a telling and cogent means by which he can launch a counterattack against those who are criticizing Yahweh's wisdom. This is especially true if Isaiah's opponents are the political wise men and court counsellors, as other Isaianic texts would lead one to suspect (cf. 29:14, 15-16; 30:1 ff.; 31:1 ff.; 5:19).[97] At any rate, once Isaiah's opponents had agreed to the basic argument of the parable, it would be very difficult for them to avoid agreement with the prophet's fundamental claim—that Yahweh acted wisely and would therefore act wisely in the future. In this particular situation, it is most suitable for Isaiah to use a wisdom teaching. In fact, it shows something of Isaiah's daring, for he uses weapons that his opponents could also use. Again, it is noteworthy that Isaiah explicitly affirms that he is willing to engage his opponents on the same level. I should argue, then, that the demands of the existential situation prompted Isaiah to employ this kind of speech.

Finally, as we have seen, the parabolic form itself seems to have been an apt vehicle for giving a prognosis of hope for Judah's future. From Isaiah's perspective, Yahweh is a God who could be depended on to act wisely and consistently; so the prophet argues for the probability that Yahweh would not continue to punish Judah in the future. All in all the parable comes out as a tremendous witness to Isaiah's profound understanding of the operation of Yahweh's wise counsel in history as well as an impressive testimony to Isaiah's skill in adapting wisdom speech to fit his own purposes.

III. PROVERBIAL SPEECH

A. ISA. 10:15

> Shall the ax vaunt itself over him who hews with it,
> Or the saw magnify itself against him who wields it?
> As if a stick should wield him who lifts it,
> Or as if a staff should lift him who is not wood!

By any odds Isa. 10:5-19 is one of the most powerful and profound speeches in Isaiah; it is also one of the most complex. The major source of difficulty is found in the passage's structural tensions. How do the various parts fit together? How

---

[97] For a further elaboration of this problem, see Chapter IV.

much has editorial and redactional reworking changed the face of the speech? Is it simply a bundle of fragments tied together in a tenuous and artificial unity? Or is a more original pattern of unity at all discernible? To assess correctly the function of vs. 15 in the whole speech, one must deal at least cursorily with these questions.

In its present form the speech has several components, each of which is fairly easy to separate. Formal and content criteria reveal the major breaks: (1) a "woe" announcement in the I-form of a Yahweh speech, containing an iteration of Yahweh's commission to Assyria (vss. 5-6) and a description of Assyria's counterplan (vs. 7); (2) a speech by the Assyrian king, using rhetorical questions in which he argues that Jerusalem's fall is inescapable (vss. 8-11); (3) a prose statement concerning Yahweh's inevitable punishment of Assyria because of her overweening pride (vs. 12); (4) a speech of self-praise by the Assyrian king, recounting the ease of his many conquests; (5) a wisdom saying, or more precisely a "disputation-fable" (*Streitfabel*), containing (a) a rhetorical question of the artisan-tool type and (b) an exclamation—both of which stress the ludicrous folly of Assyria's arrogance (vs. 15); (6) an announcement of judgment against Assyria (vss. 16-19).

On closer inspection one perceives incongruities within the speech which militate against understanding the passage as an original unity.[98] First, the curious, rather misplaced position of vs. 12—not to mention its prosaic and prolix character—argues against its genuineness. The verse appears to represent a later stage of the tradition, serving now as a conclusion to vss. 8-11 and a bridge to vss. 13-14. In its present formulation, it functions almost as a capsule-like interpretation of the overall theme of the speech—that proud Assyria will fall when Yahweh is done with her. Secondly, the twofold appearance of "for he says" (vss. 8 and 13) has an editorial stamp and seems designed to conceal or close lacunae in the speech. Both phrases

---

[98] For what follows, see the standard commentaries, esp. the basic analysis of Duhm, pp. 72 ff.; for a brilliant literary-critical examination, cf. K. Fullerton, "The Problem of Isaiah, Chapter 10," AJSL 34 (1918): 170-84.

are transitional: they look back to the preceding verses (7 and 12 respectively) and introduce a royal speech which illustrates and buttresses the point made in the previous statement. Thirdly, there are incongruities within some of the subunits. For instance, vss. 8-11 display inner tensions.[99] Finally, the threat in vss. 16-19 has a very insecure relationship to vss. 5-15 —at least on the level of an original connection. The threat itself is comprised of a montage of mixed metaphors, drawing together a series of Isaianic figures scattered throughout his oracles.[100] It seems therefore that the majority of critics are correct in labeling the threat a secondary addition.

In spite of these incongruities, one must still ask the question concerning the *Gattung* of the speech. To be sure, in its present rather baroque form it falls into the category of invective-threat, but more precision than that is desirable. Since the threat, as mentioned above, has the mark of a later addition, we may set it aside in our considerations. Likewise, vs. 12 appears to stem out of a different context and is alien in position and function to the overall movement of the speech, though akin in spirit. Leaving aside, then, these seemingly secondary elements, does a more original pattern emerge?

One possibility is that the pattern of a disputation speech is visible beneath the layers of later adaptations. If this is true the passage could be understood as a full-fledged, albeit artificially contrived, dispute between a subordinate and his superior, in this case the king of Assyria and Yahweh. In support of this thesis one may note that Isaiah constructs the disputation in order to show nakedly the folly of Assyria's *hybris*. Disputational features have long been detected in the speech. J. Begrich, following the lead of H. Gunkel, named Isa. 10:8-11 as an illustration of disputation speech.[101] Moreover, H. Gressmann called Isa. 10:15 a *Streitfabel*.[102] So one could argue that these forms, heretofore recognized in isola-

---

[99] Cf. Childs, *Isaiah and the Assyrian Crisis*, p. 42.

[100] Cf. Duhm, p. 74; Kaiser, pp. 107-8 for a summary.

[101] Begrich, *Studien zu Deuterojesaja*, pp. 48 ff.

[102] H. Gressmann, *Israels Spruchweisheit im Zusammenhang der Weltliteratur* ("Alte Kulturen im Lichte neuer Forschung," VI [Berlin: Karl Curtius, 1925]) , pp. 28-29.

tion, are interrelated components of a disputation speech. The basic parts of Isa. 10:5 ff. would then follow a pattern of claim and counterclaim, argument and counterargument, a pattern fitting the essential lines of a disputation. In this light, vs. 15 serves as Yahweh's final answer to the Assyrian king's pretentious claims. It demonstrates the absurdity of his claims which involve the adoption of an improper role. The wisdom saying would then give the knockout blow in the disputation. Exposing the ridiculousness of the Assyrian's claims, it eliminates the possibility of a comeback. The climax has been reached; the dispute is over.

From a form critical perspective, the primary difficulty with this hypothesis is that it involves an extrapolation of the dominant pattern or genre from isolated and subordinate elements in the speech. Moroever, as Childs has correctly pointed out, the Assyrian speeches really do not serve as counterclaims to Yahweh's speeches, but simply illustrate the point Yahweh makes and become the reason for punishment.[103] Whatever the hypothetical original form of the speech (and a disputational pattern is conceivable), the present form is something quite different. To wrench apart the present structure of the speech in favor of a hypothetical structure lacks cogency. Therefore one must reject the theory that the genre of the speech is that of a disputation.[104]

It is wiser to leave the speech in the broad genre of the invective-threat, which Isaiah has used to indict the Assyrians of his day. While using a traditional genre, Isaiah has applied it to his own historical situation: Assyria has arrogantly transgressed the limits Yahweh had imposed on her; Assyria is therefore doomed. As Childs observes, the decisive force in shaping the oracle is Isaiah's understanding of Yahweh's plan or counsel.[105] The sharp clash between Yahweh's counsel and Assyria's intention is clearly portrayed.

In his speech Isaiah takes something of the posture of the wise man. He reflects on the problem of the conflict between

[103] Childs, *Isaiah and the Assyrian Crisis*, p. 44.
[104] *Ibid.*
[105] *Ibid.*

human and divine purposes and simply draws the inevitable conclusion: Assyria's pride will lead to destruction. That he chooses a distinctively wisdom speech to sum up the whole oracle and to give the rationale for Assyria's destruction would seem to confirm this insight into the prophet's activity.

It is self-evident that the so-called "disputation-fable" in vs. 15 is to be viewed against the broad background of popular wisdom in the ancient Near East.[106] In addition to the potter/clay sayings in Isa. 29:16 and 45:9 ff., a similar saying is present in Ahiqar: "Why should wood strive with fire, flesh with a knife, a man with [a King]?" [107] The latter, however, functions differently from the Isaiah saying: the rhetorical question serves to support didactic instruction about proper conduct before rulers. Of course, no question of interdependence is in view; all such sayings only illustrate the wide sweep of popular wisdom.

The wisdom flavor also comes out in the gnomic quality of the logic. In answering the claims of the Assyrian king, Isaiah bases his argument on knowledge available in principle to anyone in the ancient world who has insight into the nature of the world and life. The gnomic perception into the structure of reality is revealed in vs. 15. Here the folly of one who takes on an improper role is driven to its *reductio ad absurdum:* everyone knows that an instrument does not challenge its wielder. The application to Assyria is most appropriate. Isaiah, in using a proverbial saying, applies a general truth to the specific case of Assyria. Moreover, the chief thrust of the wisdom saying fits admirably the motif of the whole speech: the *hybris* that leads to a fall—a motif which, we might add, is a favorite of wisdom teaching.[108]

[106] Gressmann, pp. 28-29.
[107] ANET, p. 429.
[108] As is well known, the shattering of pride is a central theme in Isaiah (cf. 2:7 ff.; 3:16 ff.; 9:8 ff.; 10:5 ff.; 28:1 ff.). In commenting on Isa. 2:12 ff., H. Wildberger argues for the wisdom roots of the destruction of pride envisaged in the "Day of Yahweh": "Jesaja knüpft also . . . hier an ein zentrales Ideal der Weisheit an, das aber doch zugleich völlig verändert wird durch seine Transplantation in den Vorstellungsbereich des Jahwetages" (*Jesaja,* BKAT X, fasc. 2 [Neukirchen-Vluyn: Neukirchener Verlag, 1966]: 108). His arguments, however, are not completely convinc-

To summarize: the wisdom saying has an integral function in the speech. It sums up the rationale for Yahweh's punishment of Assyria and is an indirect but damning diatribe against Assyria for her arrogance. Its wisdom rootage is evident both in the form and method of argument.

B. ISA. 29:15-16

> Woe to those who hide deep from Yahweh their counsel:
>   whose acts are in the dark,
>   and who say, "Who sees us? Who knows us?"
>
> O your perversity! [109]
> Is the potter regarded as the clay?
> Can something made say of its maker,
>   "He did not make me"?
> Or something fashioned say of its fashioner,
>   "He has no sense"?

The unit (Isa. 29:15-16) is easily delimited from its immediate context. The introductory "woe" plus the change in theme indicates the fresh beginning (vs. 15). At the other end a break is also evident, where a promise oracle appears (vss. 17 ff.). Hence Isa. 29:15-16 is a well-defined unit.

Formally speaking the whole unit may be labeled a prophetic invective. The oracle lacks a concluding threat, but this is not unusual for woe oracles. E. Gerstenberger has convincingly shown that woe oracles are an independent unit form critically and may have a variety of continuations.[110]

The invective itself, however, has a number of elements, which indicate that it is a combination of different forms. The structure may be outlined as follows:

I. Announcement of Woe (vs. 15)

II. Denunciatory Exclamation (vs. 16a)

---

ing, for the widespread use of the motif of pride would seem to militate against a derivation from wisdom tradition. At any rate, Wildberger rightly stresses the radical difference in Isaiah's usage of the motif in Isa. 2:12 ff. vis-à-vis the wise man's.

[109] Though הפככם is something of a puzzle (cf. the standard commentaries), its denunciatory thrust is fairly clear from the context.

[110] E. Gerstenberger, "Woe-Oracles of the Prophets," JBL 81 (1962): 253.

III. Disputation-Fable (vs. 16b)

The combination of the disputation-fable with the "woe" reflects the amazing diversity of forms on which Isaiah draws. The "woe" apparently condemns the political intrigues of the pro-Egyptian party at the Jerusalem court (cf. 30:1-5; 31:3). The extreme folly of the counsel-makers is sharply pointed up by their "practical atheism": "Who sees us? Who knows us?" (cf. Zeph. 1:12). On the heels of the shattering exclamation that decries their twisted perspective (vs. 16a) comes a proverbial saying to overturn any counterarguments (vs. 16b). Cast in the form of a rhetorical question, it drives the logic of their claim to a *reductio ad absurdum* (as in Isa. 10:15). No retort is possible; Isaiah's case is irrefutable. In contrast to Isa. 10:15 (where the setting is artificial), it is clear that Isa. 29:16 reflects a concrete situation in which the prophet faced real opponents. The wisdom saying is particularly apropos of the high-handed claims of his allegedly "wise" opponents, who show only a fool's grasp of the ground rules of existence operative in the ancient world: to deny God's sovereignty over the world was to play the fool. Here the close parallel in Deutero-Isaiah is noteworthy:

> Woe to him who strives with his Maker,
> an earthen vessel with the potter!
> Does the clay say to him who fashions it,
> "What are you making"?
> or "Your work has no handles"?
> (Isa. 45:9; cf. Rom. 9:20)

The accent falls on the inviolability and inscrutability of the cosmic order, where God's sovereignty is axiomatic. This theme is central in the wisdom literature, as attested by both Job and Ecclesiastes.

What is significant for our purposes is the distinctly wisdom stamp of Isa. 29:16. The method and content of the argument are drawn straight from wisdom. To be sure, the prophet uses the proverbial saying in his specific prophetic task of condemning the perversity of his people. His appropriation of a wisdom saying, however, is another attestation of how often Isaiah reached into the arsenal of the wisdom tradition for weapons to combat the folly of his people.

IV. THE SUMMARY-APPRAISAL FORM

In a recent monograph on Isaiah, B. S. Childs has suggested the possibility that Isaiah may be dependent on wisdom circles for a particular speech form which Childs has named the "Summary-Appraisal Form." [111] If Childs is correct, this would add some additional support to our thesis of Isaiah's utilization of wisdom materials. Since Childs has concisely laid out most of the pertinent material, it is not necessary for me to rehearse all of it. I shall simply summarize his thesis, add some additional evidence, and offer a critique of certain aspects of his treatment.

The basic summary-appraisal form, as Childs describes it, consists of a demonstrative (זה, זאת) which introduces a summary and generalized appraisal of a unit of material. Generally a bicolon structure is used. In the vast majority of cases, the form comes at the end of the section, though this is not uniformly true. The form has a reflective, didactic bent, often containing technical wisdom language. Childs cites several specimens of the form from the Old Testament wisdom literature:

Such are the ways of all who get gain by violence;
it takes away the life of its possessors (Prov. 1:19).

This is the fate of those who have foolish confidence,
The (end of those) who are pleased with their portion (Ps. 49:14).

Such is the fate of all who forget God,
The hope of the impious will perish (Job 8:13).

Surely such are the dwellings of the ungodly,
Such is the place of one who does not know God (Job 18:21).

This is the portion of a wicked man,
The heritage decreed for him by God (Job 20:29).

[111] Childs, *Isaiah and the Assyrian Crisis*, pp. 128 ff.

This is the wicked man's portion with God,
The tyrant's inheritance from the Almighty (Job 27:13).

The similarity in all these passages is obvious. As Childs puts it: "Each time an adverbial particle makes reference to the oracle which has preceded. Each time the bicolon form is used. Again, the sentence not only summarizes the argument, but attempts to draw a larger principle from the instance cited. . . ." [112] Finally, Ecclesiastes is filled with a spate of specimens which almost give the book the sound of a monotonous litany. Time and again we hear: "This also is vanity and a striving after wind."

In addition to the evidence Childs' produces, one can cite some other parallels from Sirach:

This is what one devoid of understanding thinks;
A senseless and misguided man thinks foolishly (16:23).

All these are for good to the godly,
just as they turn into evils for sinners (39:27).

In light of all these data, the thesis of Childs seems certainly a viable possibility. I therefore concur in his judgment that the wise men sometimes had recourse to a stereotyped speech form by which to summarize and draw generalized conclusions from their speeches. His designation of the form as a summary-appraisal is an accurate description of its intention and function.

We must now turn to Isaiah and examine more closely the three passages that Childs adduces as examples of Isaiah's usage of the form (Isa. 14:26; 17:14b; 28:29). Isa. 28:29 will be taken first, since it is the clearest example. As we saw in our detailed exegesis of the whole passage (28:23-29), vs. 29a summarizes the preceding discourse on the nature and origin of the farmer's skills, and vs. 29b offers an appraisal of the quality of Yahweh's wisdom. So the verse fits nicely the characteristics of the summary-appraisal form as seen in the samples from explicit wisdom materials. Also, the technical wisdom vocabulary supports the wisdom roots of the speech. So the conclusion of Childs that Isa. 28:29 is an illustration of the sum-

[112] *Ibid.*, p. 133.

mary-appraisal form in Isaianic preaching appears to be on solid ground.

Isa. 14:26 offers another relatively clear example of the form, although it is more distinctively stamped by Isaiah's particular concerns. The verse itself is part of a larger passage which has two clearly demarcated sections. After the announcement of judgment in a Yahweh speech (vss. 24-25), there is a definite shift in style and tone in vss. 26-27. "This break," says Childs, "is marked by the demonstrative this (*zo'th*) which functions both as a bridge from the threat to vs. 26, as well as a signal for a fresh beginning." [113] Moreover, the speaker changes: it is now the prophet not Yahweh, and the latter is mentioned in the third person. What is offered is a kind of prophetic reflection on the preceding Yahweh speech: the counsel of Yahweh is seen to have implications for the whole world. Not only do "the two rhetorical questions of vs. 27 serve in effect as motivation clauses for the appraisal to provide its authorization," [114] but they also function as an indirect polemic against any and all who would seek to overturn Yahweh's counsel by their own contrary plans. To conclude: the stylized structure, the reflective tone, and the technical wisdom vocabulary serve to substantiate the suggestion Childs offers that Isa. 14:26 is still another Isaianic example of the summary-appraisal form.

In the third example (Isa. 17:14b) the argument for wisdom vintage is more problematic. To be sure, one must immediately say that the verse is a kind of summary-appraisal. My question, however, is whether the passage is correctly explained as a specimen of the summary-appraisal form that is wisdom in character. The difficulty comes in the use of the first person plural. Childs does not see this as a problem and simply notes the similarities to Isa. 14:26, most of which are certainly correct.[115] However, it is not clear-cut that there is a change of speakers in 17:14b as in 14:26. In the latter a shift from Yahweh to Isaiah is explicitly indicated; in the former a shift is not apparent, for the mere fact of the introduction of the first

[113] *Ibid.*, p. 128.
[114] *Ibid.*, pp. 128-29.
[115] *Ibid.*, p. 129.

person plural does not in itself necessitate a change in speakers but only indicates that the speaker is now identified. Presumably the prophet is the speaker throughout the passage and here identifies himself with his people. We have a similar pattern in Isa. 1:4-9, where it is clear that Isaiah is the speaker throughout and again explicitly identifies himself with his shattered people in vs. 9 with the use of the first person plural.

In contrast to Childs, I should argue that this passage is more correctly categorized as a *cultic* "summary-appraisal." Childs himself singles out a number of speeches that closely approximate the wisdom summary-appraisal in everything but the speaker (either the "we" of the community or the "I" of Yahweh is used). For example, we read in Ps. 118:23: "This is Yahweh's doing; it is marvellous in our eyes." It should be noted that the first person plural is very rare in the wise man's summary-appraisals; only in one of the passages that Childs cites is it present (Job 20:29) and even there the form of the speech has been altered a good bit. As a rule the wise man prefers to offer a summary-appraisal in the third person, hence giving it a more objective, impersonal stamp. He is an observer and records his objective reflections on the phenomena of the world. The wise man would have given Isa. 17:14b in something like the following form: "This is the portion of those who despoil the righteous; the lot of those who plunder the godly." Of course one can argue that Isaiah has simply altered the form so as to identify himself with the people. But if this course is taken, then one could argue the same for many of the other passages that Childs has eliminated from the category of the wise men's summary-appraisals.

There is a second argument against the wisdom derivation of Isa. 17:14b. When one looks at the whole speech (Isa. 17:12-14) it is clear that cultic interests are dominant. In light of this cultic strain and in light of the use of similar forms in cultic materials, it is more in keeping with the evidence to eliminate Isa. 17:14b from the category of wisdom speeches. Although the verse is similar to the wisdom summary-appraisal, it moves more clearly in the sphere of the community's confession of confidence in the face of enemy hordes.

To summarize: the available evidence would seem to support the isolation and identification of a new wisdom form which B. S. Childs has named "The Summary-Appraisal." However, since there are similar forms in cultic use, each case in the non-wisdom books must be judged on its own merits. Therefore, while I agree that Isa. 14:26 and 28:29 are excellent specimens of the wisdom form, I should differ in regard to Isa. 17:14*b* which seems to be cultic.

V. CONCLUSION

Isaiah is rich in parabolic and proverbial speech. That he borrows such speech from wisdom is testimony to its important influence. Wisdom, as typified by the examples we have examined, is a constituent feature of the Isaianic style, affecting both the structure and substance of his message. Thus he indicts Israel for the "unnaturalness" of her apostasy by means of two parables (1:3; 5:1-7). To show up the incredible folly of Assyrian and Israelite leadership and so invalidate their arrogant claims, he appropriates a distinctly wisdom method of argumentation (10:15; 29:16). To defend Yahweh's wise counsel against criticism (28:23-29), he chooses a parable about a farmer's unpretentious labors. Finally, he utilizes a wisdom form—the summary-appraisal—in at least two of his speeches (14:26 and 28:29*b*).

More is involved here than simply a scattered use of wisdom forms, for Isaiah gives us some insight into how he approaches the realities of his world. And in this regard, Isaiah as prophet is free to operate like a wise man. He reveals his dependence on their style of speech and argumentation. To him there is no dichotomy between his insight into Yahweh's character and activity gained by empirical observation of phenomena (e.g., Isa. 28:23 ff.), and that derived in a vision (Isa. 6). Such dichotomies are more a modern construct than an ancient reality. To Isaiah there was a basic unity in Yahweh's activities in "history" and in "nature" (both modern words), for both areas are viewed from the perspective of Yahweh's sovereignty.

III

Woe Oracles and Wisdom

Isaiah has far and away the greatest concentration of woes of any book in the Old Testament (Isa. 1:4, 24; 3:9, 11; 5:8, 11, 18, 20, 21, 22; 6:5; 10:5; 17:12; 18:1; 28:1; 29:1, 15; 30:1; 31:1). That they have an integral function in his message goes without saying. For our purposes they are important for three reasons. First, in light of E. Gerstenberger's[1] proposal that the woe indictment springs originally from wisdom circles, the *form* is of fundamental significance for the problem of Isaiah's relationship to the wisdom tradition. If Gerstenberger is correct, he has discovered a major source of wisdom in Isaiah, a source which would appreciably increase the importance of wisdom in Isaianic preaching. Secondly, the *content* of the woe oracles reveals some close affinities with law as well as wisdom; it is therefore necessary to raise the question concerning the sources of Isaiah's indictment of Israel. To be more specific: Does Isaiah appeal only to a uniquely Israelite legal standard by which to indict the people's sin? [2] Or does he also appeal to

[1] E. Gerstenberger, "The Woe-Oracles of the Prophets," JBL 81 (1962): 249-64 (henceforth "Woe-Oracles").

[2] This is the prevailing view in recent literature on the prophets; cf. E. Würthwein, "Amos-Studien," ZAW 62 (1950): 40 ff.; R. Bach, "Gottesrecht und weltliches Recht in der Verkündigung des Propheten Amos," *Festschrift Günther Dehn* (Neukirchen: Neukirchener Verlag, 1957), pp. 23-34; W. Beyerlin, *Die Kulttraditionen Israels in der Verkündigung des Propheten Micha* (Göttingen: Vandenhoeck & Ruprecht, 1959), pp. 44 ff.

the popular ethos, which is reflected in the wise man's teachings on right and wrong—an ethos common to the ancient Near East?[3] Finally, R. Fey[4] has argued that Amos decisively influenced Isaiah. The woe oracles play a crucial role in Fey's argument. In fact, in his opening chapter he employs the woe oracle in Isa. 5:11-13 as a test case in order to demonstrate the viability of his thesis.[5] Moreover, in the final tally of the data Isaiah's woe oracles constitute approximately one third of the textual evidence he adduces.[6] The woe oracles, then, are very important in Fey's view for establishing the dependence of Isaiah on Amos. Therefore, any interpretation of Isaiah's woe oracles must give heed to Fey's work. Although it would go beyond the bounds of this paper to analyze all the so-called points of contact between Isaiah and Amos, an examination of the alleged dependence of a number of Isaiah's woes on Amos will serve as a preliminary check for the validity of Fey's overall thesis. These three dimensions of the problem of Isaiah's woe oracles—the question of wisdom origin, the problem of law and wisdom, and the alleged Amos *Vorlage*— are inseparably intertwined, although the degree of overlap varies from text to text. Because of this intertwining, it is necessary to discuss all three dimensions in order to gain a complete understanding of Isaiah's woe oracles.

I shall discuss first the problem of the form and the origin of the woe indictment, for it should be self-evident that one must decide on the cogency of Gerstenberger's thesis before he can legitimately use the form as evidence of wisdom influence. Then I shall delineate the function of the woe oracles in Isaiah's message, with prime focus on the question of the sources of influence. Here I shall concentrate on selected woe oracles which are especially pertinent to our main interests.

[3] Cf. Gerstenberger, "Woe-Oracles," p. 262; H. W. Wolff, *Amos' geistige Heimat*, pp. 40 ff., 60.

[4] R. Fey, *Amos und Jesaja*, pp. 7 ff., 57 ff.; for a summary of his conclusions, see pp. 144 ff.

[5] *Ibid.*, pp. 9 ff.

[6] *Ibid.*, pp. 144-45.

I

A. CHARACTERISTICS OF THE FORM

Since Gerstenberger[7] has precisely analyzed the formal elements of the woe oracles, a sketch of the main lines will suffice here. What Gerstenberger calls the standard form of the woe indictment may be summed up by the following observations: (1) the woe begins the speech unit; thus any formulas preceding it are secondary.[8] (2) The woe is generally followed by an active participle (usually plural),[9] which may be continued in parallel clauses either by participles or finite verbal forms. (3) An objective, impersonal element predominates in the form, as indicated by the penchant for plural participles or third person verbs that simply describe the activities of an unspecified group of evildoers,[10] and by the general lack of any indication of speaker. (4) The woe form may have a variety of secondary continuations, including threats (Isa. 5:9, 13-14, 24; 28:2-4; 30:3-5; 31:2-3; Mic. 2:3; Zeph. 3:5), a lament (Isa. 1:4-5), proverbs (Isa. 29:16; 45:9b), rhetorical questions (Isa. 10:3, 4a; Amos 6:2; Hab. 2:7, 13), applications to world history (Hab. 2:8, 10, 16-17), etc. The break between the woe form proper and the continuation is often well marked.[11] The diversity of these continuations, in contrast to the high degree of consistency in the structure of the woe form proper, shows that the union is secondary from the standpoint of the history of the form. This observation is also confirmed by the fact that the woe form sometimes stands alone as a self-sufficient unit (cf. Isa. 5:18, 20, 21). (5) The construction of a series of woes seems to be constitutive (e.g., Isa. 5:8 ff.; Hab. 2:6 ff.).

Because of its highly stereotyped character, the prophetic woe indictment is to be demarcated from other uses of the woe

[7] Gerstenberger, "Woe-Oracles," pp. 250 ff.; cf. also the formal analyses of C. Westermann, *Grundformen prophetischer Rede*, pp. 138 ff.; H. W. Wolff, *Amos' geistige Heimat*, p. 14.

[8] E.g., Ezek. 13:3, 18; 34:2.

[9] Gerstenberger numbers 23 out of 34 cases; for statistics, see "Woe-Oracles," p. 251, note 10.

[10] Direct address is rare in the woe oracles (cf. Isa. 5:8 ff.; 10:5; 29:1).

[11] Cf. Isa. 5:9; 5:13-14; 5:24; 28:2; Mic. 2:3.

cry (e.g., laments for the dead,[12] introductions to threats,[13] expressions of revenge or excitement, etc.) .[14] Thus the prophets seem to have preserved a form in their preaching marked by a generalized and stereotyped indictment of unspecified groups of evildoers, whose behavior evoked an ominous woe. It is improbable that the prophets created the form *ad hoc*, for it is too impersonal, too unhistorical when compared with the more usual personalized, concretized forms of their preaching.[15] One may therefore raise the question: What is the *Sitz im Leben* that gave rise to the woe form?

B. THE PROBLEM OF ORIGIN

One prevalent view derives the woe from the curse, making the former a weakened form of the latter, with the original *Sitz* located in the cult.[16] This hypothesis has some strength. The structure of some of the curses bears a striking resemblance to the woe indictments: a participle following the opening curse designates the misdeed that calls forth the curse.[17] So the curse plus the participle, as in the woe form, is a self-sufficient unit. Moreover, some similarity can be observed in the content: both focus at times on social concerns.[18] At first glance, then, these similarities would seem to point to some kind of relationship.

[12] I Kings 13:30; Jer. 22:18; 34:5; cf. Amos 5:16; Ezek 30:2. Here also belongs the related formula אוי (Num. 21:29; 24:23; I Sam. 4:7, 8; Isa. 6:5; 24:16; Jer. 4:13, 31; 6:4; 10:19; 15:10; 45:3; Ps. 120:5; Prov. 23:29; Lam. 5:16). Cf. the recent article by G. Wanke, "אוי und הוי," ZAW 78 (1966) : 215-18; Wanke carefully distinguishes between אוי הוי and shows their different formal structures and functions.

[13] Exod. 13:3, 18; Isa. 3:9, 11; Jer. 13:27; 48:46; Isa. 29:1; 10:5; Zeph. 2:5; Num. 21:29; Ezek. 16:23; 24:6, 9; Hos. 7:13.

[14] Isa. 1:24; 17:12; 18:1; 55:1; Jer. 47:6; Zech. 2:10, 11.

[15] Westermann calls attention to the significant lack of the messenger formula in the preponderant share of the woes (*Grundformen prophetischer Rede*, p. 138). For our purposes it is esp. noteworthy that Isaiah consistently has the woe form without messenger formula.

[16] Cf. Westermann, *Grundformen prophetischer Rede*, p. 139. Gerstenberger criticizes this view, "Woe-Oracles," pp. 258-59.

[17] Gen. 27:29; Num. 24:9; Deut. 27:15-26; Judg. 21:18; Jer. 48:10; Mal. 1:14.

[18] Cf. Deut. 27:15 ff.

There is, however, a deep-seated difference between the two forms, which militates against a derivation of the woe from the curse. This difference revolves essentially on the axis of relative authority. The curse has an official stamp: it must normally be given by an authorized person,[19] and any indiscriminate use is expressly forbidden.[20] So it is a highly effective declaration. The woes stand as a sharp contrast: They "cannot compete with such official and powerful pronouncements. They are much more private, much more detached from the scene of evildoing, much more contemplative, much less effective." [21] An evolutionary view of a development of woes from curses, which makes the former a "weakened" form of the latter, fails to account satisfactorily for this marked difference between the two forms. It seems much more likely that the origin and development of each are to be separated.

Secondly, it has been argued that the prophets simply appropriated the woe lament which originated in the funeral rites of everyday life. "The prophet's woe," says G. E. Wright, "is . . . to be interpreted as a form of lament. Wicked people are those over whom the prophet could utter a funeral lament. They were people to feel sorry for because the judgment of God would soon fall upon them." [22] As we have already indicated, the use of the woe for mourning is certainly attested; in fact, this usage probably belongs to the most elemental stage. And it is true that the woe cry of the prophets has some degree of affinity with this elemental funeral exclamation, for as a rule wherever the woe is employed the smell of death, misfortune, and calamity hangs heavily in the air.

The advocates of this view, however, have not paid sufficient heed to the clear-cut formal differences between the prophetic woe indictment and the woe lament. The woe indictment, on the one hand, deals generally with unidentified groups of evildoers, simply categorized by their misdeeds. Usually there

[19] Cf. Gen. 27:49; 49:7; Num. 22:6; Deut. 27:14.

[20] Cf. Exod. 21:17; 22:17, 27; Deut. 18:10-11.

[21] Gerstenberger, "Woe-Oracles," p. 259.

[22] Wright, *Isaiah,* p. 32; cf. R. J. Clifford, "The Use of Hôy in the Prophets," CBQ 28 (1966) : 459 ff.

is no indication of the speaker. It has therefore a detached, impersonal, factual character. On the other hand, the woe lament is intensely personal, addressed to a specific person or group, either already deceased or under the immediate threat of death. A simplistic derivation from the funeral lament fails to account for the emergence of the highly stereotyped prophetic woe indictment. If we agree that the woe interjection has one of its most original functions in mourning rites, we need not say also that all woe forms hark back to this one origin. To do so ignores the clear-cut differences in the various woe forms and their respective functions.

A third attempt to explain the origin of the woe indictment has been offered by Gerstenberger, who suggests wisdom circles as the most solid candidate. His basic thesis is "that the woe . . . formula had its origin in the wise men's reflections about the conditions of this world." [23] H. W. Wolff, while essentially following Gerstenberger's lead, differs in that he suggests a genetic link between the woe indictment and the woe lament: With the help of the "Haupttopos der Totenklage," the series of woes was developed in the "weisheitlichen Sprache der Sippe." [24] It may be demonstrated convincingly, in his opinion, "dass man in der erziehlichen Sippenweisheit früh Taten mit bösen Folgen unter dem 'Wehe' zusammengestellt hat." [25]

In assessing the data one is tempted at first to minimize the strength of this thesis, for he is immediately struck by the paucity of woe forms in the extant wisdom literature. To cast aside the proposal for this reason, however, ignores the cumulative force of the evidence.

Gerstenberger proceeds on two main fronts. First, he uses the intense social concern of many of the woe sayings to argue that the woe form originally came out of the "popular ethos," and that there is a close affinity with wisdom forms. [26] And one must agree that there is an impressive similarity. Both woes and wisdom deal similarly with the problems of injustice, op-

[23] Gerstenberger, "Woe-Oracles," p. 261.
[24] Wolff, *Amos' geistige Heimat,* p. 16.
[25] *Ibid.*
[26] Gerstenberger, "Woe-Oracles," p. 258.

pression, and social wrongs of all sorts—in short, with anything that upsets the equilibrium of a just social order. The list includes oppression of the poor,[27] illegal acquisition of property,[28] drunkenness,[29] etc. In a word, both have a vital stake in the preservation of the social order, which issues in a fight against all evils that would violate the integrity and stability of society.

Gerstenberger, to be sure, recognizes that social justice is also a vital concern of Old Testament law.[30] However, he points up a notable contrast between law, on the one hand, and wisdom and woe oracles, on the other. The latter

do not try to preserve the old situation in a legal fashion with formulated laws; rather they deal with this problem on a more private basis, with bitter puns, exhortations, and warnings. We observe in such records the unofficial struggle against economic corruption and exploitation, not priestly or governmental regulations. The woe-form does not belong in such authoritative and sophisticated circles. It comes from the same stratum of popular ethos as do the wisdom accounts.[31]

Thus he concludes that the joint concern for social justice forges a strong link between woes and wisdom, with a sharp contrast over against law in how that concern is expressed.

When one evaluates this line of argument, it is clear that Gerstenberger banks heavily on a form critical principle: "When it comes to the point of distinguishing between realms of life and the corresponding statements of social concern, not an elaboration of *what* was *thought,* but only a close observation of *how* the concern was *expressed* can help us." [32] That the social concern is expressed differently from the legal prescriptions leads Gerstenberger to see the closest analogy with wisdom literature. To him the forms of expression indigenous

[27] For the woe oracles, cf. Isa. 5:8, 22-23; 10:1-2; Amos 6:1 ff.; for the Wisdom Literature, cf. Prov. 14:31; 17:15, 26; 18:5; 22:22; 23:10; 24:23-25.

[28] See exegesis of Isa. 5:8 ff. below.

[29] See exegesis of Isa. 5:11 ff.; 5:22-23 below.

[30] Gerstenberger, "Woe-Oracles," p. 256.

[31] *Ibid.,* p. 257.

[32] *Ibid.,* p. 225, note 24.

to this realm of life are closer to the woe sentences; therefore, he feels on solid ground in arguing for a firm analogy. One must agree with the cogency of his form critical insight— at least to the point of saying that the balance of probability tips in his favor. He seems justified, then, in using social concern as a clue for finding the *Sitz im Leben* of the woe oracles in wisdom.

Secondly, to make the primary life-setting more precise, Gerstenberger appeals to the *'ašrê* formula as evidence for an origin of the woe form in the activities of the wise man.[33] Now if *'ašrê* has a wisdom origin and if it is a genuine counterpart to the woe form, it affords considerable help in determining a wisdom *Sitz* for the woes. There is not, however, complete concord on these points. Recently W. Janzen[34] has criticized the long unchallenged antipodal relationship between woes and *'ašrês,* proposing a different life setting for the *'ašrê* formula. If his position is correct, a key element in Gerstenberger's argument is seriously undermined. Therefore, it is necessary first to evaluate Janzen's argument, in order to determine whether the *'ašrê* formula may legitimately be utilized as evidence for a wisdom origin of the woes.

Janzen builds his case against the antipodal relationship of *'ašrê* and woe on two factors.[35] First, the explicit biblical evidence is meager: Luke 6:20-26; Eccles. 10:16-17, and Isa. 3: 10-11 (the latter two by emendation) are the only biblical references that put *'ašrê* and woe in an antipodal position. (Janzen suggests that the Lukan passage may have been the root of the hypothesis in question.) Secondly, he enlists as his main argument the distribution of the two formulas in the Old Testament—the *'ašrês* predominant in the Psalms, and the woes in the Prophets.

On the surface Janzen's criticism looks convincing; nevertheless it has a certain shallowness which makes it somewhat less than devastating to the theory of the bipolar relationship

[33] *Ibid.,* pp. 260 ff.
[34] W. Janzen, "*'Ašrê* in the Old Testament," HTR 58 (1965): 216-26.
[35] *Ibid.,* pp. 220-21.

of *'ašrê* and woe. Now admittedly the explicit biblical evidence
is a slender thread that cannot bear much weight, but Janzen's
main argument on the basis of the distribution of woes and
'ašrês is not very telling; for owing to the dominant emphases
of the psalmodic and prophetic literature, we should expect
that the *'ašrês* would be more abundant in the former and the
woes in the latter. Even more crucial is that Janzen, in arguing solely on the statistical level, fails to take sufficient note
of other facets of the evidence. As we shall attempt to show,
similarity in form, content, and general tone welds a firm connection between woes and *'ašrês,* which indicates that the two
forms seem to operate originally in the same sphere. Finally,
his own positive suggestion—that the *'ašrê* formula has its
life-setting in a general human condition of desiring the state
of another and hence calling him *'ašrê* [36]—is too vague and
imprecise, failing to link this stereotyped expression with a
more clear-cut *Sitz im Leben.*

Now we must turn to the positive evidence that Gerstenberger adduces.[37] That the woe and bliss formulas operate in
the same sphere, he argues, is confirmed by the similarity in
form, content, and outlook. In some cases the parallel is exact.
Ps. 106:3 is a striking example:

> Happy are they who observe justice,
> Who do righteousness at all times.

That this *'ašrê* saying is a self-contained unit is indicated by
the clear separation in form and content from the preceding
and following verses. The form is identical to that of the
standard form of the woe oracles. The *'ašrê* plus the following
plural participles constitute a self-sufficient unit. There is no
indication of addressee or speaker. The impersonal, unhistorical element predominates. Therefore, in all points the form is
the same as in the woes.

Although many of the *'ašrês* are now filled with liturgical

[36] *Ibid.,* p. 225.
[37] Gerstenberger, "Woe-Oracles," pp. 260 ff.; cf. also Wolff, *Amos'
geistige Heimat,* pp. 17 ff.

content, there are some that show a decided social concern. Ps. 106:3 has already been referred to. Ps. 41:2 is also an apt illustration: "Happy is he who considers the poor" (cf. also Ps. 106:3; Prov. 14:21). Hence Gerstenberger's assumption is justified that a strong social concern is an indigenous feature of one group of beatitudes, just as in the woe forms.

As an additional support for the antithetical relationship of the beatitudes and the woes, we have two texts where the two forms are put in a back-to-back contrast and where both are definitely wisdom sayings[38]:

> "Happy"[39] are the righteous! It shall be well with them,
>   for they shall eat the fruit of their deeds.
> Woe to the wicked! It shall be ill with him,
>   for what his hands have done shall be done to him.
>   (Isa. 3:10-11)

> "Woe"[40] to you, O land, when your king is a child,
>   and your princes feast in the morning!
> Happy are you, O land, when your king is the son of free men,
>   and your princes feast at the proper time,
>   for strength, and not for drunkenness! (Eccles. 10:16-17)

The portrayal of the contrast between good and evil, righteous and wicked, praiseworthy and reprehensible, is a favorite device in the pedagogy of the wise man.[41] The use of the bliss formula in instruction is designed to lead the hearer into life, as opposed to the way of death.[42] The closing lines of Prov. 8 (where Lady Wisdom is addressing her sons) epitomize this function of the beatitudes in wisdom teaching:

---

[38] It must be admitted that this support by itself is weak. Also there is the problem of too easily equating אוי with הוי in a quest for the *Sitz im Leben* (on this point, see again Wanke, pp. 215 ff.).

[39] Following emendation suggested in BHK: reading אשרי for אמרו. Most commentators consider Isa. 3:10-11 as a late addition to Isaiah from one schooled in wisdom teaching.

[40] Reading אוי or הוי for אי; cf. also LXX.

[41] E.g., cf. all the righteous/wicked, wisdom/folly proverbs (see esp. Prov. 10–15).

[42] Cf. Wolff, *Amos' geistige Heimat*, p. 20.

Happy are those who keep my ways.
. . .
Happy is the man who listens to me,
  watching daily at my gates,
  waiting beside my doors.
For he who finds me finds life,
  and obtains favor from Yahweh;
but he who misses me injures himself;
  all who hate me love death. (Prov. 8:32b, 34-36)

In conclusion, Gerstenberger's main support for the same *Sitz* for the bliss and woe forms is the similarity in form, substance, and general tendency. The textual evidence is corroborative, though not decisive. Overall, however, his cumulative argument is cogent. The bliss form helps therefore to supply indirect confirmation of the wisdom life-setting of the woe form.

To summarize: in light of the available evidence, Gerstenberger's position appears highly probable. The cumulative force of his evidence is convincing. So until new evidence is brought forward we may provisionally accept his conclusion that the woe form derived originally from the circles of the wise. This conclusion must necessarily remain somewhat tentative, because the evidence is still too slender for anything approaching the certainty we should like. In lieu of a better explanation, however, Gerstenberger's thesis is the most illuminating approach to the background of the prophetic woe oracles.

II

The next step is an analysis of individual Isaianic woes. In approaching this task there are two interrelated questions to keep in mind. One—and this will be our central focus—is the question of traditional *sources*. In accepting as a working hypothesis a wisdom origin for the woe form, we should naturally expect wisdom to be retained as one traditionary source. Since wisdom influence on Isaiah is our dominant interest, this source will have the lion's share of attention. However, since the woe forms are now in a prophetic context, there are other traditionary sources from which Isaiah could conceivably draw in order to fill the old woe forms with new content. Other than wisdom, we shall be principally concerned with two other potential sources: Old Testament law and Amos. All these areas, of course, may in some measure overlap. Our chief concern will be delineating the source which has the most immediate and dominant influence.

The second question is that of *function*. That is, what is the role of the woe oracles in Isaiah's message? How much have his preformed, inherited materials helped to shape the profile of the woe oracles? On the other hand, how much have his own concerns dominated the speech? This dialectic between the "old" and the "new" must be delineated as sharply as possible in order to determine the degree of Isaiah's indebtedness to his traditionary heritage as well as his creative reshaping of a traditional genre.

It is relatively easy to describe the woe speeches in which Isaiah's stamp is most evident, for his own distinctive concerns come strongly to the fore. Here a brief description will suffice. In several instances the woes function as a stringent indictment of the apostasy of Yahweh's people—thus highlighting the parlous state of Israel's relationship with Yahweh. One only has to line up a series of woe oracles to see this particular Isaianic (and prophetic) concern:

> Woe sinful nation
>   a people laden with iniquity,
> offspring of evildoers,
>   sons who deal corruptly! (1:4a)

> "Woe to the rebellious children,"
>   say Yahweh
> "who carry out a plan, but not mine;
> and who make a league, but not of my spirit,
>   that they may add sin to sin;
> who set out to go down to Egypt,
>   without asking for my counsel,
> to take refuge in the protection of Pharaoh,
>   and to seek shelter in the shadow of Egypt!" (30:1-2)

> Woe to those who go down to Egypt for help
>   and rely on horses,

who trust in chariots because they are many
and in horsemen because they are very strong,
but do not look to the Holy One of Israel
or consult Yahweh! (31:1)

The latter two woe oracles have apparently been shaped by Isaiah's opposition to the faithless political ventures of the pro-Egyptian party within the Jerusalem court. The historical situation is concrete and specific. Isaiah's mark is also clear in terminology: for example, the use of one of his favorite terms (counsel) and his distinctive title for Yahweh (the Holy One of Israel). Also, the particular concerns of Isaiah's existential situation are reflected in Isa. 29:15-16, where a proverbial saying is used in the invective against those on whom the woe is pronounced.[43] Finally, Isaiah's particular interests are evidenced in his announcement of woe against Assyria (10:5), Ephraim (28:1), and Ariel (=Jerusalem, 29:1).

Over against these woe speeches we find a second series of woes which contain condemnations of perennial social and human sins—indictments less specifically Isaianic, and more stereotyped and typical. These appear to preserve reproaches that are older and more original than the woes we just described. The latter are much more pointed and concrete, bound inextricably to the political and religious crises of Isaiah's day. Thus Gerstenberger seems correct when he concludes: "'theological' concerns in woe sentences appear to be secondary; 'social' concerns, however, must be integral and original."[44] This second group includes the following: 5:8, 11, 20, 21, 22; 10:1-2. To be sure, this group of woes is still shaped in varying degrees by Isaianic concerns, as will presently be shown. However, since they have retained to a higher degree older and more stereotyped reproaches, they are especially pertinent for delineating the sources of influence on Isaiah's

---

[43] One could also include here the woe saying in 5:18-19 with its quotation from Isaiah's opponents which expresses their skepticism concerning Yahweh's counsel and work. For an exegesis of Isa. 5:18-19; 29:15-16; 30: 1 ff.; 31:1 ff. from another perspective, see below Chapter IV.

[44] Gerstenberger, "Woe-Oracles," p. 225, note 24.

preaching. It will be our purpose to give a more detailed analysis of this second group of woes.

A. ISA. 5:8-10

> Woe to those who join house to house,
> who add field to field;
> until there is no more room,
> and you are made to dwell alone in the midst of the land.

> Yahweh of hosts has sworn in my hearing;
> "Surely many houses shall be desolate,
> large and beautiful houses, without inhabitant.
> For ten acres of vineyard shall yield but one bath,
> and a homer of seed shall yield but an ephah."

Isa. 5:8 ff. is an excellent point of entry for our exegesis of selected Isaianic woes, for it is paradigmatic of our central focus: the problem of Isaiah's traditionary sources. First of all, is there a specialized, uniquely Israelite legal precedent involved? Or does the indictment express only the broad ethical backdrop of the popular ethos similar to that reflected in the wisdom texts? Secondly, is there a special dependence on Amos?

Commentators[45] have generally assumed the specific background of the legal prescriptions in the Pentateuchal Law Codes. The text to which appeal is often made is Lev. 25:8 ff., a passage dealing with property rights as dictated by the law of the Jubilee Year. In keeping with a precise legal context, the prescriptions are quite specialized. Vs. 23 may be viewed as a summation of the legal principle behind the Jubilee Year regulations concerning the land: "The land shall not be sold in perpetuity, for the land is mine" (Lev. 25:23a). This law shows that the land could not be disposed of as private property for the simple reason that it was in reality Yahweh's possession which he had given in trust to the Israelites. In principle, then, the Israelite "owners" of the land did not have the power to buy and sell the land in perpetuity. The Jubilee Year legislation provided that the land, if sold, would revert to the clan to which God had originally given it (Lev. 25:8 ff.).

---

[45] E.g., Kaiser, *Der Prophet Jesaja*, pp. 47:48; Wright, p. 32; H. Wildberger, *Jesaja*, BKAT X, fasc. 3 (Neukirchen-Vluyn: Neukirchener Verlag, 1968) : 183-84.

Isaiah's woe is thus explained as an indictment of those who were violating this legal principle of the covenant society. The woe oracle in Mic. 2:1 ff., which shows that the unjust monopolistic acquisition of land was not just a problem to Isaiah, is interpreted similarly and used by W. Beyerlin as evidence to support his thesis that Micah relied heavily on the cultic law of the old amphictyony.[46]

In comparing these two woe sentences with Lev. 25:8 ff., it is questionable whether it is justified to read them in light of the cultic regulations of Leviticus. To be sure, both sets of texts evidence a deep concern for the poor; no one would deny that in this respect both prophetic indictment and Levitical legislation ultimately have the same roots.[47] However, when the woes are placed side by side with the priestly law, a contrast is readily apparent: the latter is a specific legal prescription, couched mainly in casuistic legal form; on the other hand, the woes contain only a general condemnation of unjust amassing of property. Nothing is said of the specialized legislation connected with the Jubilee Year, nor is any explicit mention made of Yahweh's ownership of the land. Hence no tight lines can be drawn to this kind of traditionary background without undue stretching of the texts. The point is this: the unlawful seizure of property violates age-old ethical rules indigenous to any sedentary society; no precise cultic prescriptions were requisite to understand the onus of Isaiah's condemnation.

Acceptance of the wisdom origin of the woe indictment gives the best explanation of the popular stamp of Isaiah's condemnation. Biblical and ancient Near Eastern wisdom texts are full of warnings and exhortations about property rights, in particular the rights of the poor. For example, we read in Egyptian *Instructions:*

> Do justice whilst thou endurest upon earth. Quiet the
> weeper;

[46] Beyerlin, p. 59.
[47] Cf. Gerstenberger, *Wesen und Herkunft des "apodiktischen Rechts,"* where he discusses the *Sippenethos* as the source of the social concerns of both law and wisdom (pp. 10, 110 ff.) . See also Richter, pp. 148 ff.

supplant no man in the property of his father.[48]

> Do not carry off the landmark at the boundaries of the
>   arable land,
> Nor disturb the position of the measuring-cord:
> Be not greedy after a cubit of land,
> Nor encroach upon the boundaries of a widow.[49]

> Be not greedy for the property of a poor man.[50]

The biblical wisdom texts display the same concern for property rights. Job's "friends" describe his alleged wickedness with these words:

> For he has crushed and abandoned the poor,
> he has seized a house which he did not build. (Job 20:19)

> The man with power possessed the land,
> and the favored man dwelt in it. (Job 22:8)

Similarly, Proverbs is replete with warnings against acts of greed:

> He who oppresses the poor to increase his own wealth,
> or gives to the rich, will only come to want. (Prov. 22:16) [51]

> Do not remove an ancient landmark
> or enter the fields of the fatherless. (Prov. 23:10;
>   cf. 22:28)

It is important to note that the same tone pervades these wisdom texts as we found in the woe indictments. The texts are based on age-old rules that are concerned with the protection against the avaricious and power-hungry.

Indirect confirmation for the rootage of Isaiah's woe indict-

---

[48] ANET, p. 415.

[49] Ibid., p. 422.

[50] Ibid., p. 423.

[51] The concern for the poor is a dominant concern of Wisdom literature (cf. Prov. 14:31; 17:5a; 19:17; 21:13; 22:8a; 22:22; 28:3a; 29:7; 30:14; 31:9). This same concern is held in common with all the legal and wisdom materials of the ancient Near East (cf. F. C. Fensham, "Widow, Orphan, and the Poor in Ancient Near Eastern Legal and Wisdom Literature," JNES 21 [1962]: 129-39).

ment in the popular ethos is found in Hab. 2:6 ff.[52] There we find similar woe words applied to the realm of world history, specifically leveled against the rapacious Chaldean ruler. The same criteria of judgment are applied to him as were applied by Isaiah (and Micah) to an Israelite audience; both are condemned at the same bar of judgment. Thus we hear:

> Woe to him who heaps up what is not his own—
> for how long?—and loads himself with pledges. (2:6)

> Woe to him who gets evil gain for his house,
> to set his nest on high, to be safe from the reach of harm!
> (2:9)

No uniquely Israelite law was required to condemn avaricious seizure of property—it was reprehensible in any ancient Near Eastern society. So we conclude that the rules of the popular ethos—reflected in the wisdom texts—lay behind Isaiah's indictment, not a special cultic and covenant law peculiar to Israel.[53] To be sure, the fact that Isaiah was condemning a people bound to Yahweh in a covenantal relationship made all the more reprehensible their violation of fundamental ethical rules.

R. Fey accepts a distinctively Israelite legal precedent for Isa. 5:8-9, but he attempts to go beyond this kind of general influence and posits Isaiah's special dependence on Amos. To name a few samples of the type of proof he presents:[54] (1) The apparently intrusive second person plural in Isa. 5:8b is attributed to the stylistic influence of the Amos *Vorlage* (Amos 5: 11a). (2) Isaiah's reproach of "those who join house to house, who add field to field" is simply an appropriation of Amos 5:11, 12a. (3) Isaiah's threat—that those who gain riches un-

---

[52] Wolff uses the terms in the caption to this series of woes as proof of the wisdom derivation of the woe form; he lists the *Stichwörter* מליצה, משל, and חידות as characteristic of wisdom (cf. Prov. 1:6) (*Amos' geistige Heimat,* p. 22). This line of argument is not wholly convincing, for such terms sometimes attract materials that are not truly wisdom in origin; e.g., משל is often used in the sense of "taunt" (cf. Isa. 14:4); see Eissfeldt, *Der Maschal im Alten Testament,* pp. 52 ff.

[53] On this question, cf. also W. Richter, pp. 148 ff.

[54] Fey, pp. 59 ff.

justly will not be able to enjoy them—is traced back to Amos 5:11*b*. (4) In Isa. 5:10 the concept of decimation is borrowed from Amos 5:3. (5) Fey describes the threat about the destruction of the houses (Isa. 5:9*b*) as a reworked and expanded version of Amos 3:15*b* and 6:11—it is, he goes on to say, "einer der stärksten Beweise, dass Jesaja die Amossprüche sehr genau kannte und geradezu systematisch nach zusammengehörigen Worten absuchte." [55]

On the other hand, whenever Isaiah differs from his *Vorlage*, this is interpreted as the manifestation of Isaiah's independence vis-à-vis his prophetic master.[56] For instance, when Isaiah adds the words עד אפס מקום (5:8*b*), he is going beyond Amos and pressing the thought to a conclusion *ad absurdum*. Moreover, to Fey the word לבדכם demonstrates Isaiah's penetrating insight into the true nature of the people's transgression: instead of Yahweh *alone* it was the landowners *alone;* Yahweh, the true Owner of the land, had been displaced! So Fey concludes:

> With this theological concentration of the reproach, Isaiah here as in 5:11-13 independently moves beyond his *Vorlage*. He breaks through the purely social mode of observation, by which the legal complaint is expressed in Amos, and places the transgression in direct relationship to the original regulation of Yahweh.[57]

I have recited Fey's position at some length in order to illustrate his method of handling the problem of Isaiah's relationship to Amos. Although one may admit the general similarity of Isa. 5:8 ff. with certain of Amos' oracles, it is dubious that this really constitutes convincing evidence of a *special* dependence. First, the content of the invective/threat here is simply too common to warrant the kind of conclusions Fey draws.[58] Similarity alone does not insure dependence. Fey's method seems almost to involve a "bookish" kind of literary dependence. Secondly, the way Fey jumps from text to text in Amos in order to assemble his proof is very suspicious. At times

[55] *Ibid.*, p. 60.
[56] *Ibid.*, p. 61.
[57] *Ibid.*
[58] We have only to compare Mic. 2:1 ff. where both the form and content closely approximate Isa. 5:8 ff.

Isaiah's speeches are construed as a patchwork of expressions from Amos. Finally, to explain the differences as simply illustrative of Isaiah's independence from his *Vorlage* is too convenient; one can sidestep the problem of divergences in this way. In conclusion, it is more likely in light of the data that Isaiah and Amos have similarities because of analogous situations and common traditions. So we must reject Fey's interpretation of Isa. 5:8-10 in terms of the special influence of Amos.

B. ISA. 5:11-13

> Woe to those who rise early in the morning
>   that they may run after strong drink,
> who tarry late in the evening till wine inflames them.
> They have lyre and harp,
>   timbrel and flute and wine at their feasts,
> but they do not regard the deeds of Yahweh
>   or see the works of his hands.
> Therefore my people go into exile for want of knowledge;
>   their honored men are dying of hunger,
>   and their multitude is parched with thirst.

The topic of drunkenness crops up frequently in Isaiah (Isa. 5:11, 22; 22:13; 28:1, 3, 7; 29:9). That it is also a common motif in wisdom texts is amply attested (Prov. 20:1; 21:13; 23:20-21; 23:29 ff.; 31:4 ff.; Eccles. 10:16-17; Sir. 19:2; 31:25-31). Prov. 23:29-35 is illustrative of wisdom teaching on the woes of wine. It is especially useful as a point of comparison with Isa. 5:11-13, for it enables one to perceive both the affinity and divergence of a typical wisdom lesson and a prophetic invective.

> Who has woe? Who has sorrow?
> Who has strife? Who has complaining?
> Who has wounds without cause?
> Who has redness of eyes?
> Those who tarry long over wine,
>   those who go to try mixed wine.
> Do not look at wine when it is red,
>   when it sparkles in the cup and goes down smoothly.
> At the last it bites like a serpent,
>   and stings like an adder.
> Your eyes will see strange things
>   and your mind utter perverse things.

You will be like one who lies down in the midst of the sea
like one who lies down on the top of a mast.
"They struck me" but I was not hurt;
they beat me but I did not feel it.
When shall I awake? I will seek another drink.
(Prov. 23:29-35)

Following the lead-off questions, comes the brief answer:
"Those who tarry long over wine//who go to try mixed wine"
(23:30). The burden of the speech is the prohibition (vs. 31)
to which is added the motivation (vss. 32-35). The latter is
made up of a description of the detrimental effects that wine
leaves in its wake. The didactic intent is revealed in the question-answer form as well as the typical wisdom description of
the debilitating course that drunkenness naturally follows.
Here too, as in most of the wisdom warnings against drunkenness, the problem is viewed as a threat to one's personal happiness.

This passage is an apt foil against which to set Isaiah's handling of the same theme. In correspondence to the woe plus
participle (5:11), the sage has the related formula אוי in a
question form (with other synonymous terms) and the plural
participles in the answer (23:30). The same word מאחרים is
used in both passages to describe the activity of those on whom
the woe comes. Also, the effects of the wine are somewhat
similarly portrayed: vision is impaired and knowledge deficient. **142094**

The differences are no less striking and depict vividly the
radicalized nature of the prophetic message. Instead of the
didactic question-answer scheme (למי אוי), there is a somber
pronouncement of woe. Instead of describing how wine ad-
versely affects the physical senses, Isaiah penetrates to the
deepest level of spiritual insensitivity: "They do not regard
the deeds of Yahweh, or see the work of his hands" (5:12b).
Here was the real failure in knowledge. Finally, instead of
presenting only a warning, the prophet announces doom (vs.
13). On all these counts Isaiah's handling of the theme tran-
scends the sage's, for the prophet zeroes in on the detrimental
effect of extravagant living at the point of its implications for

the people's relationship to Yahweh: "My people goes into exile for lack of knowledge" (vs. 13a; cf. also 1:3). Therefore, though a common theme of wisdom is visible in Isaiah's indictment, he goes far beyond wisdom in theological concentration.

As already indicated, Isa. 5:11 ff. is a test case in Fey's thesis of an Amos *Vorlage* for Isaiah.[59] To be sure, Fey also recognizes that Isaiah holds his theme in common with the wisdom tradition, but the Amos *Vorlage* (Amos 6:1-7), in his opinion, is a more decisive determinant of the contours of Isaiah's woe oracle. Fey's evidence is based on form and content. Both passages follow a similar invective-threat pattern in which a woe introduces the invective and a לכן the threat; both have a longer *"Vordersatz"* (Amos 6:1-6a; Isa. 5:11-12a) and a short, negative *"Nachsatz"* (Amos 6b and Isa. 5:12b); both are stylistically similar in their alternation between participles and finite verbal forms; and both portray the judgment in terms of exile.

On the surface such evidence may appear compelling, but it is deficient at a key point: all the data he adduces are too common to warrant his judgment that they demonstrate a special dependence of Isaiah on Amos. For instance, the use of the woe indictment followed by a threat introduced by לכן is not unusual.[60] Also, the stylistic argument—the several changes from participle to finite verbs—is common in woe speeches.[61] It is especially suspect when one considers that Fey builds his argument on the assumption that Amos 6:1-6 is a formal unity. This is an unwarranted assumption, for there are internal difficulties that militate against such a unity. For instance, it is possible that a woe has dropped out at the beginning of vs. 4.[62] If this be true, it would mark a seam in the

[59] For what follows, see Fey, pp. 12 ff.

[60] E.g., Isa. 5:24; Mic. 2:3.

[61] Gerstenberger, "Woe-Oracles," p. 252.

[62] E.g., cf. RSV translation; also there is a problem how vs. 2 fits into the unit. At present it is formed of a plural imperative (2a) and a question (2b) which has a didactic bent. At any rate, the sudden switch back to a participle in vs. 3 shows that there are stylistic and formal incongruities within the passage. This fact should cause one to be cautious about building too much on an argument from style.

unit. Therefore any use of a stylistic argument dependent on the unity of the passage must be held in suspicion. Finally, as well as not giving full heed to the common elements from general prophetic tradition, Fey has not given due regard to the common wisdom theme—drunkenness—on which both prophets seem dependent.

In light of the evidence, it is much more likely that both Amos and Isaiah were using traditional materials (the woe form, the theme of drunkenness), each prophet leaving his own mark on the materials. So Amos excoriates the people for not being grieved at the ruin of Joseph (Amos 6:6b), whereas Isaiah gives the indictment his own characteristic turn: the people have failed to discern the work of Yahweh (Isa. 5:12b). Fey's view, then, is not convincing since it ignores the common aspects of the traditional materials Isaiah and Amos utilize and does not pay full heed to the divergences. For this reason, we must reject his explanation of the influences on Isaiah's woe oracle.

C. ISA. 5:22, 23

> Woe to those who are heroes at drinking wine,
>   and valiant men in mixing strong drink,
> who acquit the guilty for a bribe,
>   and deprive the innocent of his right!

In this strongly ironic indictment of excessive drinking, Isaiah links the drunkenness motif with social injustice. Those who engage in "heroic" feats of drinking are the very ones who perpetrate injustice in judicial proceedings. Here it is men of influence, those in the position of rendering judgments, who are condemned.

Although some commentators want to separate vss. 22 and 23, there is no sufficient reason for doing so. That there is a transition in theme from drunkenness to perpetration of injustice is no real problem. In fact, an intrinsic connection between the two themes is also made in a wisdom text:

> It is not for kings, O Lemuel,
>   it is not for kings to drink wine,

or for rulers to desire strong drink;
lest they drink and forget what has been decreed,
and pervert the rights of all the afflicted. (Prov. 31:4-5;
cf. also Eccles. 10:16-17)

The thematic parallel is quite close and helps to confirm not
only the original connection of the two verses in Isaiah, but
also shows again the wisdom affinities of the woe speech.[63]

R. Fey transposes vs. 23 into a genetic relationship with vs.
20 on the grounds of thematic continuity and then argues that
both verses are dependent on Amos. The passages on which
vs. 23 is allegedly dependent are Amos 5:7b: "Those who cast
down righteousness to the earth," and Amos 5:12b: "Those
who afflict the righteous, who take a bribe, and turn aside the
needy in the gate." To support his case Fey cites three cor-
respondences: the similarity in the concept of צדקה; the use of
צדיק; and the topic of bribery.

Again the evidence militates against Fey's thesis, as ably
demonstrated by H. W. Wolff.[64] The latter adduces data that
point to the wisdom tradition as a more adequate source for
Isaiah's speech. Isaiah's use of צדקת צדיק has a close analogue
in wisdom speech; so we read in Prov. 11:5, 6:

The righteousness of the blameless (צדקת תמים)
keeps his way straight,
but the wicked falls by his own wickedness.
The righteousness of the upright (צדקת ישרים)
delivers them,
but the treacherous are taken captive by their lust.

Also, these proverbs show that the concept of righteousness as a
protective power, used by Fey to argue for a dependence on
Amos, is held in common with their broader background of
wisdom. Wolff rightly concludes: "Here Isaiah, like Amos, in
his usage of language and mode of conceptualization is to be
understood directly from wisdom." [65]

[63] See above the remarks on Isa. 5:11 ff. concerning the wisdom background of the drunkenness motif.
[64] For what follows, see Wolff, *Amos' geistige Heimat,* pp. 56-57.
[65] *Ibid.,* p. 56.

Wolff employs the same method of argument against Fey's citing of the bribery motif as further proof of special dependence.[66] The use of the phrase, "who justify the wicked" (רשע מצדיק) has an exact parallel in Prov. 17:15 and a close analogue in Prov. 24:24:

> He who justifies the wicked (מצדיק רשע)
> and he who condemns the righteous
> are both alike an abomination to Yahweh. (Prov. 17:15)

> He who says to the wicked, "You are righteous" (אמר לרשע צדיק אתה)
> will be cursed by peoples, abhorred by nations.
>   (Prov. 24:24)

Moreover, Isaiah uses a different word for bribery than Amos: שחד and כפר, respectively. שחד may belong to the speech of the court (cf. II Kings 16:8); if so, Isaiah's use of it here and in connection with the court officials (1:23) would be understandable.

To summarize: the thematic connection of drunkenness and social injustice has a firm parallel in wisdom teaching and seems to be rooted there. The evidence fails to justify Fey's arguments for a close dependence of Isaiah on an Amos *Vorlage*. On the contrary, it further corroborates the case for a wisdom background for Isaiah's woe speech.

D. ISA. 5:20

> Woe to those who call evil good and good evil,
> who put darkness for light and light for darkness,
> who put bitter for sweet and sweet for bitter!

Isa. 5:20 is interesting for two reasons: (1) it reflects the didactic background of contrasting word pairs and, in using this technique, the overall social concern of the woe speeches; (2) it is another element in Fey's argument for an Amos *Vorlage*.

I shall begin with Fey. First of all, he links vs. 20 and vs. 23 into a kerygmatic unity—which, as we indicated above, is an

---

[66] *Ibid.*, p. 57.

unnecessary and unwarranted move.[67] In any case, to him the resultant unit illustrates Isaiah's creative appropriation of kerygmatic elements from Amos, to which the former gives a new profile.[68] The basic idea of the reversal of ethical values הפך (Amos 5:7a) is picked up and further developed by Isaiah (vss. 20, 23). Moreover, the antithetical word pairs in vs. 20 are attributed to Amos' influence: good/evil (Amos 5:14-15); light/darkness (Amos 5:18-20); sweet/bitter (Amos 5:7a; cf. 6:12b). Also, another striking proof for Isaiah's indebtedness to Amos is the lack of a threat, just as in the supposed Amos prototype (Amos 5:7, 10, 12b). Again, Fey describes Isaiah's "freedom" with his *Vorlage*. Whereas light and darkness are concrete and literal in Amos, they become ethical categories in Isaiah: "Isaiah no longer speaks of the dark or bright day, but of 'works of darkness' and 'unsullied acts.' Out of disparate individual elements Isaiah fuses a new unity in sharp profile." [69]

Fey's employment of Isa. 5:20 as evidence of Isaiah's dependence on Amos is indefensible for several reasons. First, he creates an artificial unity with vs. 23 to make the alleged connection with Amos stronger. Simply because the two verses have the same movement of thought is no reason to transpose them into a single unit. Secondly, Fey's argument that the lack of threat constitutes proof of Isaiah's dependence on his *Vorlage* is unconvincing, since the woe sentence was originally an independent form critical unit.[70] Finally, his use of contrasting word pairs is very tenuous; these pairs are far too general to be used as evidence of a special influence of Amos. It is more probable that such contrasts have a general didactic background. At any rate, their very commonness militates against the way Fey uses them. We must therefore reject Fey's hypothesis of Amos' influence on Isa. 5:20.

Our last criticism of Fey is a good place to begin a positive explication of Isa. 5:20. As we indicated, it is more likely that

[67] Fey, p. 57.
[68] *Ibid.*, pp. 58-59.
[69] *Ibid.*, p. 59.
[70] Gerstenberger, "Woe-Oracles," p. 253.

the antithetical word pairs reflect a didactic bent which is especially evidenced in wisdom teaching. Wisdom delights in contrasting wise/foolish, good/evil, righteous/wicked, light/darkness, etc. in order to delineate sharply the ways of death and the ways of life.[71] These and other opposites crowd the pages of the wisdom literature. For example:

Hatred stirs up strife//but love covers all offenses.
(Prov. 10:12)

Whoever loves discipline loves knowledge//but he who hates reproof is stupid. (Prov. 12:1; cf. 13:24)

Do they not err that devise evil?
Those who devise good meet loyalty and faithfulness.
(Prov. 14:22)

He who is sated loathes honey,
but to one who is hungry everything bitter is sweet.
(Prov. 27:7)

These examples show that the woe sentence has the same didactic tendency, and help to confirm the broad wisdom background of the speech.

Isaiah's use of this woe word summarizes his condemnation of those who were disrupting the social order and reversing those values that were endemic to a sound society. Again, these values were not derived from cultic pronouncements or special revelations, but were rooted in the popular ethos, with the best analogy in wisdom teaching.

E. ISA. 5:21

Woe to those who are wise in their own eyes,
and shrewd in their own sight.

Pride is a recurring motif in wisdom, especially that pride which exulted in self-wisdom. The perils of such pride loom large in wisdom teaching:

When pride comes, then comes disgrace;
but with the humble is wisdom. (Prov. 11:2)

[71] Cf. Wolff, *Amos' geistige Heimat*, pp. 46 ff.

Pride goes before destruction,
 and a haughty spirit before a fall. (Prov. 16:18)

Haughty eyes and a proud heart,
 the lamp of the wicked are sin. (Prov. 21:4)

Pride and arrogance and the way of evil
 and perverted speech I hate. (Prov. 8:13b)

Even more striking is the phraseological similarity of Isaiah's woe speech with the speech of wisdom. The expression "wise in one's own eyes" is a stereotyped phrase that occurs often in Proverbs:

Be not wise in your own eyes. (Prov. 3:7a)

Answer a fool according to his folly,
 lest he be wise in his own eyes. (Prov. 26:5)

The sluggard is wiser in his own eyes
 than seven men who answer discreetly. (Prov. 26:16)

Do you see a man who is wise in his own eyes?
 There is more hope for a fool than for him. (Prov. 26:12)

A rich man is wise in his own eyes,
 but a poor man who has understanding will find him out.
 (Prov. 28:11)

This exact parallel with wisdom teaching confirms the wisdom backdrop of the woe word.

That this woe has a timeless, ahistorical quality is easy to see: woe, according to wisdom, would always come ultimately upon anyone who was foolish enough to be "wise in his own eyes." It is, however, legitimate to raise the question whether Isaiah had a more specific application in mind. In light of his persistent condemnation of Judah's statesmen for "going it alone," with a cocksure confidence in the wisdom of foreign alliances, it does not seem amiss to link the woe saying with this specific political background (cf. Isa. 30:1 ff.; 31:1 ff.). To be sure, only the larger context of Isaiah allows one to make this connection; hence it is only implicit.[72]

[72] Interpreters are split on whether or not to make this more specific application. Cf. below Chapter IV for an analysis of Isaiah's conflict with the political wise men at the Jerusalem court.

In conclusion, the significant thing for our purposes is that the woe saying displays a definite wisdom orientation and helps to corroborate Gerstenberger's illuminating insight about the wisdom roots of the woe oracles.

F. ISA. 10:1-2

> Woe to those who decree iniquitous decrees,
> and the writers who keep writing oppression,
> to turn aside the needy from justice,
> and to rob the poor of my people of their right,
> that widows may be their spoil,
> and that they may make the fatherless their prey!

In this woe oracle Isaiah again turns against those who are responsible for the administration of justice and indicts them for a blatant failure in their responsibilities. The exact identity of those who "decree iniquitous decrees" and "write oppression" is uncertain.[73] The participles $hqqm$ $mktbm$ do not seem to designate particular offices. Nevertheless it is clear that Isaiah is reproaching the leading circles of his people, and some type of royal officials is no doubt meant. This would square with other Isaianic speeches in which the prophet hurls invectives against the leaders of Judah, especially those responsible for social justice (1:23; 3:14-15; 5:23).

G. Fohrer has attempted to specify more exactly the group in question by asserting that it is comprised of those officials who are trained in the wisdom school.[74] W. Richter has also recently used Isa. 10:1-2 (along with other texts) to argue for the thesis that a wisdom school existed in Jerusalem, one of whose primary tasks was the instruction of officials in duties of just leadership.[75] If this view is correct, Isaiah would be indicting the leaders on the basis of an ethos upheld and taught by the wise men as well as the lawgivers. Richter is reflecting the new understanding of wisdom and law which sees both going back to common roots. In my judgment, his position

[73] But cf. Wildberger (*Jesaia*, p. 98) who thinks $hqqm$ designates a royal office.
[74] Fohrer, p. 92.
[75] Richter, pp. 149-50.

represents an accurate reading of the material. To be sure, his thesis of a special court school is not completely convincing since the evidence he cites is very indirect and so inconclusive.[76] It is more in keeping with the evidence to stick with Gerstenberger's notion of the popular ethos rather than postulate the existence of a school. The important point, however, is that Richter's book is further confirmation of the intimate relation of wisdom and law and illustrates the complexity of the heritage on which Isaiah draws.

Now we must turn to Isa. 10:1-2 in order to delineate more clearly the relationship between Isaiah and his traditions. The very movement of the woe indictment makes it clear that the fundamental purpose of the promulgation of decrees is the oppression of the poor (vs. 2). This concern for the poor pervades all the main strata of the Old Testament—whether law, wisdom, or prophets. It was especially the responsibility of the king to insure protection of the weak and defenseless of society (cf. Ps. 72; Isa. 11:4). Such a dominant and pervasive motif reflects the common roots of wisdom and law, and it is unwise to distinguish too closely between law and wisdom in the search for the particular traditionary background on which the prophet is drawing the material for his indictment. It is noteworthy, however, that a close parallel in content to this indictment—Isa. 3:13-15—seems to draw on wisdom teaching to make the basic charge. In form Isa. 3:13 ff. is a trial speech.[77] It is the central accusation that is of central interest to us: "It is you (i.e. elders and princes) who have devoured the vineyard/the spoil of the poor is in your houses" (3:14b). As in Isa. 10:2 (cf. also Mic. 2:2), Isaiah condemns the ruling classes for robbing the poor. Now robbing one's neighbor is explicitly prohibited in legal sentences (cf. Lev. 19:13; 5: 21 ff.). But it is a wisdom admonition that comes the closest to Isaiah's accusation:

[76] Cf. Gerstenberger's similar criticism in his review of Richter's book (JBL 86 [1967]: 490).

[77] Cf. Boecker's analysis, *Redeformen des Rechtslebens im Alten Testament*, pp. 84 ff.

Do not rob (*'l-tgzl*) the poor, because he is poor,
or crush the afflicted in the gate;
for Yahweh will plead their case
and despoil of life those who despoil them. (Prov. 22:22-23)

As Wildberger notes, "The similarity in the formulation allows no doubt that the agreement is not accidental: Isaiah in his diction closely follows instructions as imparted by wisdom to officials." [78] Although I would not state the matter so apodictically, I think Wildberger is essentially correct in seeing a reflection of wisdom teaching in Isaiah's reproaches. At least, Isaiah is indicting the ruling classes on the basis of an ethos upheld by the wise men. Hence the ruling classes were condemned by criteria which the prophet could presuppose that the former knew both from legal prohibitions and wisdom admonitions. So whether one emphasizes the legal or the wisdom background of Isaiah's indictments, the common roots of wisdom and law are highlighted.

To conclude: The evidence seems clearly to favor the understanding of law and wisdom exemplified in the works of Gerstenberger and Richter. Though one cannot be absolutely certain, the wisdom background seems to be more evident in these two Isaianic indictments (3:14b and 10:1-2). In the latter passage, if the wisdom derivation of the woe form is correct, the wisdom roots of the content would be even more understandable.

III

I must now summarize the chapter and attempt to draw some conclusions. Although I dealt with only one speech genre (the woe indictment), I raised a number of different questions which led to different conclusions. First of all, the evidence seems to favor Gerstenberger's thesis concerning the wisdom origin of the woe indictment. Though the data are not so clear and unambiguous as one would like, nevertheless the cumulative force of the arguments is cogent. Moreover, in the

[78] Wildberger, *Jesaia,* p. 133.

analysis of the pertinent Isaianic woes, the *content* often showed strong affinities with wisdom materials. So it seems that Isaiah has preserved still another wisdom *Gattung* in his message.

Secondly, the chapter had implications for the highly complex problem of wisdom and law. Though it was not my purpose to enter into a full discussion of this problem, my exegesis of selected woe oracles confirmed Gerstenberger's thesis that Isaiah is relying on the rules of the popular ethos in his indictments of social wrongs. One simply cannot make a strong case for a rigid separation between wisdom and law, asserting that the latter is somehow uniquely and distinctively Israelitic and so superior to wisdom. Rather the rules in legal sentences and wisdom teaching go back to the same soil, even though they are developed and transmitted in different forms and settings. To be sure, much is still obscure, especially in the matter of the different kinds of *Sitz im Leben*. For instance, Richter's thesis of a special wisdom school which was responsible for the instruction of those in the ruling class is too tenuous in light of the available evidence, though it is an enticing possibility. At any rate, my analysis of the Isaianic texts supports the work of Gerstenberger and Richter, both of whom have made notable advances in dispelling romantic notions of the origin and nature of Israelite law vis-à-vis wisdom.

Finally, I utilized the woe oracles as a means of testing R. Fey's thesis of a special dependence of Isaiah on an Amos *Vorlage*. When judged on the basis of the evidence adduced from the woe oracles (which again amounts to a third of the textual evidence he cites), Fey's thesis is found wanting. It is more in keeping with the data to see both prophets indebted to common sources of tradition than to posit a relationship of special dependence, though of course this is not to rule out absolutely any dependence.

IV

Counsel/Counsellor and Jerusalem Court Wisdom

I. THE NATURE OF THE PROBLEM

It has long been recognized that the term "counsel" (yā'aṣ/
'ēṣā) plays a stellar role in Isaiah's message.[1] In fact, the concept of Yahweh's counsel or plan is a primary datum of Isaianic
preaching and is one of his most distinctive contributions to
Israelite prophetism. For our purposes, his usage of the term
is highly important. First of all, it seems to be a technical
wisdom term. If one can show clear-cut connections between
Isaiah's use of yā'aṣ/'ēṣā and the wise man's, he has gone a long
way in demonstrating the thesis that wisdom has decisively
influenced Isaiah. Secondly, Isaiah's employment of the term
is intimately joined with the problem of Isaiah's political outlook, especially as shaped by his conflict with the court wise
men and political counsellors. It serves therefore as an excellent springboard for a discussion of wisdom and politics in
Isaiah's message.[2]

[1] The most comprehensive analysis is still that of J. Fichtner, "Jahwes
Plan in der Botschaft des Jesaja," ZAW 63 (1951) : 16-33. Now reprinted
in Gottes Weisheit: Gesammelte Studien zum Alten Testament ("Arbeiten
zur Theologie," 2. Reihe, Band 3 [Stuttgart: Calwer Verlag, 1965]), pp.
27-43.
[2] This problem has most recently been treated in McKane's Prophets
and Wise Men, pp. 65 ff. For an excellent discussion of the whole problem
of prophets and politics, see N. K. Gottwald, All the Kingdoms of the
Earth (New York: Harper & Row, 1964).

It is obviously insufficient, however, simply to observe that *yā'aṣ/'ēṣā* has its primary provenance in wisdom and then conclude *ipso facto* that Isaiah betrays wisdom influence. Although some scholars have been content to do this,[3] it is an oversimplification at best and fails to elucidate Isaiah's particular usage of the term vis-à-vis the wise man's. The problem is much more complex and cannot be solved by such sweeping generalizations. Only when one can demonstrate precisely the kind and degree of wisdom influence in Isaiah's usage of *yā'aṣ/* *'ēṣā* will he be able to talk convincingly of Isaiah's appropriation and adaptation of a *wisdom* term.

To clarify the various dimensions of the problem, it is instructive to glance at the most important suggestions in previous research which illustrate common approaches to the problem. First of all, Fichtner has written two important studies which impinge on our topic. As we recall in his article, "Jesaja unter den Weisen," he proposed the thesis of Isaiah's dependence on wisdom traditions; as a part of his evidence he cites Isaiah's use of *yā'aṣ/'ēṣā*.[4] Unfortunately, he does not really go beyond the mere mentioning of the term; so the treatment is hardly sufficient. In the second article, "Jahwes Plan in der Botschaft des Jesaja," he discussed comprehensively the function of *yā'aṣ/'ēṣā* in Isaianic preaching.[5] Here again, however, Fichtner does not explicate the precise relationship between Isaiah's usage of the term and the wise man's. In my judgment, Fichtner has not successfully carried through his earlier insight of Isaiah's indebtedness to wisdom, for he failed to make a sufficient analysis of the specific lines connecting Isaiah with the wise—in the present case, Isaiah's utilization of what is apparently a technical wisdom term.

Secondly, G. von Rad offers an interesting suggestion on the traditional roots of the term vis-à-vis Isaiah's adaptation. The term "is secular in origin, and signifies the decision arrived

[3] E.g., J. Fichtner, "Jesaja unter den Weisen," TLZ 74 (1949), cols. 75-80; see now the reprint in Fichtner, *Gottes Weisheit*, pp. 18-26, esp. p. 23.

[4] *Ibid.*

[5] Fichtner, *Gottes Weisheit*, pp. 28 ff.

at in a council. Very probably what is thought of is the royal council in heaven, in which a political project was discussed and then resolved upon (I Kings 22:19-22)." [6] To von Rad, then, the connection of the secular term with Yahweh is very likely the prophet's own creation, albeit done probably against the backdrop of the mythological tradition of Yahweh and his heavenly council. Von Rad concludes: "This idea of a plan to which Jahweh gives effect in history is a new element in the preaching of the eighth-century prophets." [7]

Von Rad's suggestion is appealing. The concept of the mythological background of the heavenly council is a viable possibility for interpreting *part* of the traditional rootage of Isaiah's use of the term. In my estimation, however, von Rad has overlooked important evidence in the wisdom traditions for explaining Isaiah's use of this *particular* term. Until this evidence is brought into the picture, von Rad's interpretation, while suggestive, is nevertheless deficient.

Finally, the most recent treatment of the problem is found in W. McKane's *Prophets and Wise Men,* which exemplifies a long popular approach to the whole question of the relationship between prophets and wisdom and is therefore illustrative of a larger trend. Basing his interpretation on an understanding of wise men and prophets as irreconcilable opponents, McKane argues that Isaiah appropriated wisdom vocabulary in order to combat the sages' pretentious claims and apply to Yahweh alone the prerogatives that the sages claimed for themselves.[8] Although McKane's explanation has some elements of truth, it is vitiated by oversimplification and a faulty appraisal of the wisdom traditions. Not only does McKane fail to explain adequately the function of $y\bar{a}^c a\d{s}/^c\bar{e}\d{s}\bar{a}$ in the Isaianic context, but he does not recognize sufficiently the complexity of the wisdom sources available to Isaiah. The

---

[6] G. von Rad, *Old Testament Theology* II: 162. On the subject of the heavenly council, cf. the basic treatments by H. W. Robinson, "The Council of Yahweh," JTS 45 (1944) : 151-57; F. M. Cross, Jr., "The Council of Yahweh in II Isaiah," JNES 12 (1953) : 274-77; E. C. Kingsbury, "The Prophets and the Council of Yahweh," JBL 83 (1964) : 279-86.

[7] G. von Rad, *Old Testament Theology* II: 162.

[8] McKane, pp. 65 ff.

latter accounts for the oversimplified dichotomy between Isaiah and the wise men. That there is a difference is indubitable. Nevertheless, McKane, as I shall attempt to demonstrate below, has not drawn an accurate portrait of that difference and has thereby failed to appreciate both the profundity of Isaiah's adaptation and the rich complexity of the wisdom traditions.

These samples of scholarly opinion show that before one can really talk about Isaiah's usage of the term in relationship to the wise man's, he must determine the understanding of "counsel" in wisdom circles. First, the understanding of what is involved in *human* counsel must be clearly grasped. Who gave counsel? What was the view of the authority of the counsel? What sorts of presuppositions were involved in the counsel-making process? Secondly, what about the question of a *divine* counsel? What place did a divine counsel play in the wise man's world view? How did the wise man view his counsel vis-à-vis God's? These questions underscore a fundamental fact: what is new and distinctive in Isaiah's utilization of $y\bar{a}'as/'\bar{e}s\bar{a}$ will only emerge with any kind of clarity when the nature of his traditionary sources is delineated. Understanding the whence of the term will help to explain the why of Isaiah's use of it.

II. THE WISDOM BACKGROUND OF YĀ'AṢ/'ĒṢĀ

The wisdom provenance of our term is summed up in Jeremiah's famous quotation of the words of his adversaries: "Come, let us make plots against Jeremiah, for the law shall not perish from the priest, nor counsel ($'\bar{e}s\bar{a}$) [9] from the wise,

---

[9] The translation of $y\bar{a}'as/'\bar{e}s\bar{a}$ is somewhat problematic. The translations are usually either "counsel/advice" or "plan/purpose." Fichtner makes an over-rigid distinction between these two meanings, although he recognizes there is a relationship between them in that the counsellor has a plan in mind when he gives counsel and calls for a definite decision (Fichtner, "Jahwes Plan in der Botschaft des Jesaja," *Gottes Weisheit*, p. 29). McKane rightly criticizes this over-fine distinction, esp. in Fichtner's faulty conclusion that Isaiah uses the term differently from the narrator of such passages as II Sam. 15:12, 31, 34; 16:20, 23; 17:7, 11, 14, 15, 21, 23.

nor the word from the prophet" (Jer. 18:18b). According to the prophet, counsel is as decisive for the wise as the Torah is for the priest and the Word for the prophet. Although the quotation is from the seventh century B.C., there is little doubt that it would be an accurate presentation of the terms that best exemplify the three circles represented by prophet, priest, and wise man.[10] A similar picture is given in Isa. 19:11:

> The princes of Zóan are utterly foolish;
> the wise counselors of Pharaoh give stupid counsel.

To minimize this separation between "counsel" and "plan," McKane proposes the translation " 'policy' which indicates that 'ēṣā is advice with a view to action" (p. 66). The difficulty with "policy" is that it is too official and is more apropos of the contexts that reflect a political *Sitz im Leben*. In my judgment, "counsel" gets closest to the basic meaning of the root, since "counsel" may not only refer to the advice given by the counsellor to the counsellee, but also may connote the idea of plan or design. In fact, any "counsel" always presupposes the prior formulation of a plan which is designed to lead to a definite course of action. The difficulty with the translation "plan" is that it may be construed to mean a firmly fixed program which is valid for all times irrespective of the situation. This would be a false conception of 'ēṣā, for the activity of the one engaged in the formulation of 'ēṣā is always strongly conditioned by the exigencies of the particular situation. In the final analysis, however, it is only the context that will fix the exact nuance of meaning, and this sometimes requires different English words. To be sure, one must bear in mind that the Hebrew writer uses the same word whereas we may be forced to use several different words; so it is incumbent upon the translator to be alert to the common preunderstanding that lies behind the Hebrew writer's use of the same word in different contexts.

[10] It is still disputed whether the "wise" in this passage refers to a definite class of wise men or is simply to be identified with the leaders. (For the most recent survey of the data with a representative selection of the secondary literature, see Richter, *Recht und Ethos*, pp. 187-88.) For our purposes, what is decisive is that "counsel" is associated with a group called the "wise"—whatever the exact makeup of the group. It should be said, however, that to identify the wise simply with the leaders is too imprecise, since the wise men along with princes (שרים), judges (שפטים), elders (זקנים) were all counted as leaders. I say this with the awareness that it is often difficult to draw precise differences between the functions of the various types of leaders, since the functions sometimes overlap, but this does not overturn the fact that there were differences. And the scattered references in the historical books and pre-exilic prophets seem to point clearly to the presence of a class of wise men—at least in the Jerusalem court—from the days of Solomon on (cf. among others the survey of McKane, pp. 55 ff.).

How can you say to Pharaoh,
"I am a son of the wise,
a son of ancient kings"?

The passage is of uncertain vintage and date (most scholars consider it non-Isaianic) ; so it cannot be used as direct and unambiguous evidence for Isaiah's understanding of the wisdom background of counsel/counsellor. Also, the description is of the Egyptian court and cannot be used as direct testimony of the situation in the Jerusalem court. Nevertheless it is indicative of the widespread notion of the close link between the counsellor and wisdom circles and shows the close relationship between counsellors and the royal court.

Furthermore, the overall statistical evidence lends strong support to the predominant wisdom background of our term.[11] To be sure, there was a certain overlap. For example, just as a prophet[12] or wise man[13] could give Torah on occasion, so counsel could sometimes be given by prophets,[14] priests,[15] princes,[16] or elders.[17] It should be noted that in almost every case it was only an authoritative person who could give counsel and that this was often done in the context of deciding important political questions at the royal court.[18] In the majority of cases, however, it was the wise man who dispensed counsel, either in his general role in the community,[19] or in his more

[11] Cf. the complete survey of the biblical texts in the comprehensive study of P. A. H. de Boer, "The Counsellor," VTS 3 (1955): 42-72. A thorough form critical and traditio-historical study of $y\bar{a}'a\d{s}/'\bar{e}\d{s}\bar{a}$ is still sorely needed in order to arrive at a precise and accurate understanding of the *Sitz im Leben* and functions of this term. See now, however, J. R. Irwin, "The Revelation of עצה in the Old Testament" (unpublished Ph.D. Dissertation, Drew University, 1965). (Inaccessible to me; see *Dissertation Abstracts* 26 [1965/66], p. 7470.)

[12] Cf. II Kings 17:13; Isa. 1:10.

[13] Cf. Prov. 3:1; 4:2; 6:23; 7:2; 13:14; Job 6:24.

[14] I Kings 1:12; cf. II Chron. 25:16.

[15] Exod. 13:19.

[16] Ezek. 11:2.

[17] I Kings 12:6 ff.; Ezek. 7:26.

[18] Cf. P. de Boer, p. 56: "[counsel] is a decision in a difficult situation given by an authorized person. . . ."

[19] Cf. Job 5:13; 26:3; 29:21; Prov. 1:25, 30 (Lady Wisdom as Counsellor) ; 12:15; 20:18.

official role as a member of the royal court where he had the formal title "counsellor" (*yôʿēs*).[20] It was in the latter capacity that the wise man's presence is felt in Isaiah (but more about this later).

Whereas wide agreement exists on the wisdom background of *ʿēsā*, its basic *character* is a topic that triggers vigorous debate. Here one runs head on into the complex problem of the definition of older wisdom in Israel,[21] for one's conception of wisdom in large measure determines his view of counsel. So it is necessary at least to touch on the larger problem where it impinges on the clarification of the nature of the wise man's counsel.

One group of scholars tends to label the wise man's *ʿēsā* as originally a secular, humanistic term—which is a simple consequence of their definition of older wisdom.[22] Since McKane is the latest representative of this widely held view, I shall take his position as paradigmatic. McKane posits a rigid distinction between the secular and the religious spheres, the wise man (at least in older wisdom) working in the former and the prophet in the latter.[23] In the context of the Israelite Kingdom, the wise man became the counsellor par excellence who applied his critical acumen to the problem of politics. McKane envisages this "old wisdom" as "a disciplined empiricism engaged with the problems of government," [24] whose "ideals are . . . intellectual honesty, rigour, and probity. . . ." [25] Moreover, by definition this wisdom is bereft of any ethical or religious

[20] Cf. II Sam. 15:12, 31, 34; 16:20, 23; 17:5 ff.; I Chron. 26:14; 27:32, 33; Ezra 7:28; 8:25; Isa. 1:26; 3:3; 19:11, 17 (cf. also Isaiah's portrait of the Messiah, 9:5; 11:2); Mic. 4:9; Job 3:14; 12:17; Prov. 11:14; 15:22; 19:20; 20:18; 24:6. On this function of the counsellor, see de Boer, p. 57; McKane, pp. 55 ff., 65 ff., and finally the thorough description of the courtly background of wisdom in H. Duesberg's and I. Fransen's *Les scribes inspirés* (rev. ed.; Belgium: Maredsous, 1966), pp. 147 ff., esp. 167 ff.

[21] For the most recent and comprehensive review of the problem, see Schmid, *Wesen und Geschichte der Weisheit*, pp. 141 ff. Cf. also Murphy's summary in CBQ 29 (1967): 407 ff.

[22] E.g., K. Zimmerli, "Zur Struktur der alttestamentlichen Weisheit, ZAW 51 (1933): 183; McKane, pp. 55 ff., 65 ff.

[23] McKane, pp. 65 ff.

[24] *Ibid.*, p. 53.

[25] *Ibid.*, p. 47.

commitment, for the wise men "were persuaded that the world in which they had to operate . . . was not amenable to the assumptions of religious belief or to a black and white ethical terminology." [26] In fact, the wise men, as McKane paints them, were dead set against any religious or doctrinaire policy: "In their professional capacity they thought it right to challenge the encroachment of religious authority on their sphere of responsibility, for they argued that they had to reckon realistically with political existence and to deal faithfully with the world as it was and not as it ought to be." [27] In this understanding of wisdom, the sage's counsel therefore was dependent on his ratiocinative faculties and its authority solely contingent on the cogency of his logic. Any reference to God was therefore out of the question.

So long as one holds such a view of wisdom and counsel, it is easy to see how Isaiah's usage of *'ēṣā* was simply explained as an appropriation and radical reinterpretation of wisdom vocabulary in order to combat the *secularistic* policy of the sages.[28] Isaiah's view of Yahweh's *'ēṣā* was interpreted as an *ad hoc* creation for polemical purposes. To be sure, McKane argues that Isaiah poured a positive content into it, but there were really no positive antecedents in the wisdom tradition.

The winds of change, however, have been blowing for some time and for a growing number of scholars wisdom has taken on a different look from that of McKane's presentation. Indeed, what is surprising about McKane's monograph is that he leaves his flank seriously exposed by failing to reckon more adequately with recent insights into ancient Near Eastern wisdom. The weaknesses of his approach will emerge in our exposition of some of the more notable advances in wisdom research.

First and foremost, McKane does not deal with the basic concept of an order in the world, which seems to have formed a crucially important presupposition in the wise man's ap-

[26] *Ibid.*
[27] *Ibid.*
[28] *Ibid.*, "The Attack on Old Wisdom," pp. 65 ff.

proach to reality.[29] The wise man took this order—created and guaranteed by God—as the starting point in his attempt to master life. Of course the view of this order varied from culture to culture. For instance, in Egypt this order was intimately connected with the concept of *Maat*.[30] But in Israel, too, the wise man recognized a basic order in the world. Time and again the Proverbs reflect a cognizance of this order, especially in the correlation of act and consequence.[31] To be sure, in the process of discovering this order, the wise man worked primarily with the stuff of basic experience; his was the concern to find out the underlying order in the world by means of looking and listening.[32] However, the wise man realized that ultimately the world order was not at his disposal, that he could not penetrate to its innermost core, and that God alone had full insight into the order of the world in all its aspects.[33] In other words, the wise man reckoned with the fact that God alone was the Creator and Controller of the world. To say that the wise man was completely an independent, empirical operator, as McKane does, is to misread the data of ancient wisdom and view it through the lens of a modern construct. The wise man always reckoned with God—who loomed up in his experience as a limiting factor, as one who exercised ultimate control. For instance, scattered throughout the book of Proverbs are the following sayings:

> A man's mind plans his way,
> but Yahweh directs his steps. (Prov. 16:9)

Many are the plans in the mind of a man,

[29] Cf. G. von Rad, *Old Testament Theology* I: 421 ff.; Gese, *Lehre und Wirklichkeit in der alten Weisheit*, pp. 33 ff.

[30] Cf. Gese, pp. 1 ff.; A. Volten, "Der Begriff der Maat in den ägyptischen Weisheitstexten," *Las sagesses du Proche-Orient ancien*, pp. 73 ff.; H. Brunner, "Der freie Wille Gottes in der ägyptischen Weisheit," *Les sagesses du Proche-Orient ancien*, pp. 103 ff.

[31] Cf. the following sayings in Prov. 10:2, 4, 30; 11:21; 12:11, 14; 13: 25; etc.

[32] E.g., Prov. 15:31; 24:30 ff., esp. vs. 32: "Then I saw and considered it//I looked and received instruction."

[33] Cf. Prov. 15:3, 11; 16:2; 17:3; 20:27; 21:2; 24:12.

but it is the counsel of Yahweh (*'āṣat yhwh*) that will be
established. (Prov. 19:21)

A man's steps are ordered by Yahweh,
how then can man understand his way? (Prov. 20:24)

No wisdom, no understanding, no counsel (*'ēṣā*)
can avail against Yahweh.

The horse is made ready for the battle,
but the victory belongs to Yahweh. (Prov. 21:30, 31) [34]

Such wisdom, as von Rad puts it, "combines two things—man's
confidence in his ability to master life and at the same time,
with all the wisdom in the world, an awareness of the frontiers
and a preparedness to fail in the sight of God." [35]

It is against this broader background of wisdom that the
counsel-making process must be understood. Now, to be sure,
there is a wide area of agreement on basic elements in the
makeup of the wise man's counsel, and it is not necessary for
our purpose to go into a complete analysis of the term.[36] For
instance, all would agree that the wise man's counsel was based
on a careful assessment of the situation and drawn primarily
from his store of experience. His counsel, however, was ultimately grounded in his perception into the *divinely*-created
order, so that it is a mistake to speak of a purely empirical
approach, as McKane tries to do. "The insights attained into
the world around her," argues von Rad, "were in the last
analysis orders apprehended by faith." [37] And again: "In the
unyielding assumption that in spite of all there must be an
order in things was already inherent an implicit faith ac-
quainted with the deep hiddenness of the divine *conservatio*
and *gubernatio*." [38]

The wise man's counsel was not bereft of authority, for it

---

[34] One should observe that this is not a distinctly Israelite attitude, but
is also present in the ancient Near East; note the Egyptian saying in
Amen-em-opet 19:16: "One thing are the words which men say, another
is that which the god does" (ANET, p. 423).

[35] G. von Rad, *Old Testament Theology* I: 440.

[36] Cf. again de Boer, pp. 42 ff.

[37] G. von Rad, *Old Testament Theology* I: 427.

[38] *Ibid.*

had implicitly the authority of God behind it, because of its rootedness in the divinely created order. Also, if de Boer's explanation of counsel as a "decision that determines the future" is correct, this authority is increased.[39] Of course, the elements of the inner logic of argumentation and the expertise in speaking also contributed to the authority of the counsel (e.g., the Ahithophel-Hushai debate in II Sam. 17). At any rate, an understanding of counsel as non-authoritative must account for *all* these elements in the character of counsel; if it fails to do so, a faulty view results—whether it be based on the highly tenuous presupposition of a "pure empiricism" or the "anthropocentric-eudaemonistic starting-point of wisdom."[40]

Although the wise man understood his counsel as having authority, he nevertheless recognized the limits of that authority. These limits hinge upon the ultimate impenetrability of the order of the cosmos and especially the incalculable sovereignty of God. As we indicated already, the wise man perceived that God was ultimately in control and that human counsel could be overruled. It is sometimes argued that it was *only* the prophets who put the wise men in their place by stressing Yahweh's overruling sovereignty. That the prophets had some stinging remarks on this point is true,[41] but it is wrong to see this as a uniquely prophetic condemnation. We have previously cited a number of proverbs that demonstrate the wise men's healthy respect for God's superintendence in human affairs (cf. again, Prov. 16:9; 19:21; 21:30, 31). Some scholars still want to maintain that such proverbs represent a later injection of Yahwistic faith into the bloodstream of the wisdom movement in order to bring the secular body of wisdom more in accord with the religious community of Israel.[42] This position should once and for all be rejected as a hangover from the days when the wisdom movement was viewed as an evolutionary development from the secular to the

---

[39] P. de Boer, p. 56.
[40] Zimmerli, "Zur Struktur der alttestamentlichen Weisheit," p. 203.
[41] See below our exegesis of the pertinent Isaianic texts.
[42] See note 22.

religious. Such an a priori can no longer stand up in light of the recent study into the nature of wisdom in the ancient Near East.[43] The prophets are not innovators at this point, although they condemn the wise in no uncertain terms for forgetting the limits of their wisdom and counsel. As we shall see below, this crisis in wisdom, in Isaiah's eyes, is a constituent element in the whole crisis in eighth-century Judah.

As further evidence that the wise men were well aware of the limits of human counsel, I cite two other literary works which had their origins in the early Jerusalem court and which were both apparently influenced by wisdom: The Court History of David, and the Joseph Story. That they both antedate Isaiah is important in establishing the nature of the wisdom tradition available to Isaiah.

In the Court History of David, there are several references to the activity of counsellors, most of which are bunched together in the narratives comprising chapters 15–17 of II Samuel. The portrayal of the process of counsel-making found therein may be considered paradigmatic of what went on in the royal court from the days of David to the end of the monarchy. The context of these chapters is the revolt of Absalom. In the chaos during David's retreat, David sends back loyal Hushai in order to defeat the counsel of Ahithophel (II Sam. 15:34). The latter had a stellar rating—his counsel was comparable to an oracle of God (II Sam. 16:23). The next scene is in Absalom's council chambers, where Ahithophel and Hushai are pitted against one another. Although both men present skillfully their respective counsels, Absalom and his advisers opt for Hushai's— which ironically is the worst counsel. At this point the narrator interjects his theological explanation of what was really determinative in the proceedings of the council: "Yahweh had ordained to defeat the good counsel (*'āṣat*) of Ahithophel so that Yahweh might bring evil upon Absalom" (II Sam. 17: 14*b*). Although God does not actively intervene, he yet controls the events, even when it requires overturning good coun-

[43] See note 21.

sel.[44] The emphasis is the same as in the proverbs mentioned previously. It should cause no surprise that the Court History was written in the Solomonic era, where wisdom was one of the dominant influences in the so-called Solomonic "enlightenment." [45] Although the evidence does not permit one to speak of direct wisdom influence on the narrator, one can say that wisdom was certainly instrumental in shaping the total context in which such a work could be written. It is not remiss to say that the understanding of the limits of the wise man's counsel over against God's intention was certainly a constituent element in the intellectual environment of the royal court, for the view of the proverbs and that of the author of the Court History are too similar to be fortuitous. According to the writer of the Court History, Yahweh can and does superintend in human affairs and even overturn the wise man's counsel when it is contrary to the divine purpose. To this the court wise men could only agree.

The Joseph Story contains even more impressive and explicit evidence that the early wise men were well aware of the mysterious interplay of human and divine purposes. It has become generally accepted that von Rad is correct in his thesis that the Joseph narrative is a "didactic wisdom-story," whose *Sitz im Leben* is in the period of the early monarchy.[46] Indeed, to von Rad, the story is a parade example of early wisdom writing. In the story Joseph is presented as a model of the wise man's educational ideal, who epitomizes the best qualities in the wise man's teaching. In his role as administrator in Pharaoh's court, Joseph is the master counsellor, skilled in

[44] Cf. the observation of M. Noth: "Die befremdliche Tatsache aber, dass Absalom den Rat Ahitophels verwarf, beruhte auf einer Wirkung Jahwes, der durch eine solche Lenkung eines menschlichen Entschlusses den Geschichtsverlauf so führte, wie es seinem Willen entsprach" ("Die Bewährung von Salomos 'göttlicher Weisheit,'" VTS [1955]: 237).

[45] G. von Rad has brilliantly described the impact of this era on historical writing, esp. the altered views of the way God works in history ("The Beginnings of Historical Writing in Ancient Israel," *The Problem of the Hexateuch and Other Essays*, pp. 166-204).

[46] G. von Rad, "The Joseph Narrative and Ancient Wisdom," *ibid.*, pp. 292-300; also his *Die Josephgeschichte* ("Biblische Studien," Heft 5 [Neukirchen: Neukirchener Verlag, 1964]), pp. 11 ff.

speech and cogent in counsel. The foundation of his wisdom is "the fear of the Lord" (Gen. 42:18).

For our immediate interests, the significant element in the story is the explicitly drawn contrast between human intentions and the divine direction of history. The key statement is found in Joseph's speech of comfort to his brothers: "As for you, you intended (*ḥăšabtem*) evil against me; but God intended (*ḥăšābāh*) it for good . . ." (Gen. 50:20). According to von Rad this statement is the climax of the whole story and reflects in the most concentrated fashion the theology of early wisdom.[47] Recognized with sharp clarity is the limitation of human intentions and the ultimate sway of God's sovereignty. To von Rad, "this opposition between the divine economy and human intentions is a central issue in the theology of wisdom-writing." [48] He even suggests that our sentence in Gen. 50:20 may be a "wisdom-saying which has been adapted to the purpose of the story." [49] Again, the similarity of the statement to some of the Proverbs cannot be missed; e.g.;

> A man's mind plans his way,
> but Yahweh directs his steps. (Prov. 16:9)

> Many are the plans in the mind of a man,
> but it is the counsel of Yahweh that will be established.
> (Prov. 19:21)

It is very important to observe that the thought in the Court History, the Joseph Story, and the Proverbs, is not only a negative one—human counsel is limited; but also a positive one—God has a plan in history. And this plan is effected in the course of human events and through human instrumentality. Hence it is my thesis that the wise men in the Jerusalem court possessed in their *own* traditions the recognition of a divine counsel which took priority over any human plans or counsels. It is important to underscore that both the Joseph Story and the Court History of David have their *Sitz im Leben*

---

[47] G. von Rad, *Die Josephgeschichte*, p. 20.
[48] G. von Rad, "The Joseph Narrative and Ancient Wisdom," *The Problem of the Hexateuch and Other Essays*, p. 297.
[49] *Ibid.*

in the Jerusalem court and so reflect the theological under-standing of the *royal* wise men. It seems, then, a fundamental mistake to argue, as McKane and others, that the court wise men were simply disciplined empiricists, who ruled out any consideration of the divine factor. Rather it is more accurate to say that the court wise men at Jerusalem—from the days of Solomon on—were most cognizant of the notion of a divine purpose which could limit and even overrule their counsel. Indeed, it was a hallmark of wisdom to recognize this fact and the height of folly to deny it. And this was the kind of wisdom tradition present at the Jerusalem court and available in principle to Isaiah.

If what we have said is correct, the implications for Isaiah's usage of the motif of Yahweh's *'ēṣā* versus man's are highly important. We may now make a provisional statement of these implications, the nuances of which will be delineated in the exegesis of the pertinent Isaianic passages. First of all, it seems clear that Isaiah worked against the backdrop of a court wisdom that had as an intrinsic part of its traditions the recognition of the mysterious interplay of Yahweh's coun-sel and man's. The way Isaiah argues against the wise men would certainly suggest this (cf. Isa. 28:23 ff.; 29:15-16), and therefore would match the view of human and divine counsel we have seen in the older wisdom represented by Proverbs, the Joseph Story, and the Court History of David.

Secondly, the data would suggest that Isaiah not only bor-rowed the wisdom terminology (*yā'aṣ/'ēṣā*) per se, but also appropriated the concept of *Yahweh's 'ēṣā* from the wisdom traditions. As we shall see, Isaiah's view of Yahweh's counsel which is materialized in history has strong affinities to the view expressed in the older court wisdom (e.g., compare only Gen. 50:20 and Prov. 19:21 with Isa. 14:24 ff.). To be sure, there are obviously some differences, but the point is that the terminology and the conceptuality reflect a similar traditionary background. What we apparently have is another illustration of Isaiah's reactualization of a motif from older traditions, although his adaptation is typically prophetic. That there were other traditionary forces at play in Isaiah's formulation of the concept of Yahweh's purpose is certainly possible. For instance, there is some likelihood that the mythological background of Yahweh's kingship and the heavenly council exerted some influence on Isaiah's concept of Yahweh's purpose.[50] But this would not be strange in light of the close relationship between court and cultic traditions in Jerusalem, and it is not at all surprising to see both strains in Isaiah's message.

Finally, Isaiah's stringent condemnation of the wise men (e.g., Isa. 29:14, 15-16) is not distinctly prophetic. Rather it is based on criteria drawn from the wise men's *own* traditions. The wise men of Isaiah's day were reprehensible on the grounds of their *own* understanding of what constituted true widsom; they were guilty before their *own* bar of judgment.

The cumulative evidence drawn from the book of Proverbs, the Court History of David, and the Joseph Story seems, in my opinion, to confirm the nature of the wisdom traditions that would be known by Isaiah as he worked within the context of the Jerusalem court. Also, as I shall attempt to show, the explicit wisdom materials in Isaiah which talk either about Yahweh's counsel (e.g., Isa. 28:29) or the court wise men's counsel (e.g., Isa. 29:15-16) seem to jibe with the picture given in the older wisdom. We must now turn to the Isaianic passages in order to confirm our preliminary observations and to interpret the ways in which Isaiah adapted his wisdom traditions.

III. THE FUNCTION OF COUNSEL/COUNSELLOR IN ISAIAH

As I have indicated, the fundamental analysis of this topic is still that of Fichtner in his article, "Jahwes Plan in der Botschaft des Jesaja." In his valuable treatment, Fichtner's basic question was different from mine, for he concentrated on the whole issue of a divine plan in Isaiah. So he was not principally concerned with the question of wisdom influence in Isaiah's formulation of the concept of a divine plan, even

---

[50] G. von Rad, *Old Testament Theology* II: 162.

though *yāʿaṣ/ʿēṣā* was the main term by which Yahweh's plan was expressed. However, Fichtner's examination must be the starting point of any analysis of the function of counsel/counsellor in Isaiah, despite the different shape of his question. His basic thesis[51] was that Yahweh's plan primarily involved a divine judgment for Israel and the nations, although salvation for God's people stood in the background. Isaiah announced Yahweh's plan to his people, but they refused to take his message seriously (5:12, 19) —this despite the impact of the initial effects of the plan (5:12; 22:11; 9:7 ff.). The plan or work of Yahweh was characterized as "strange" and "alien" (28:21*b*), "marvellous" and "wonderful" (29:14; cf. 28:29). The plan did not simply involve Israel, but embraced the whole earth (14:26; 28:22), especially Assyria which played the crucial role of Yahweh's instrument of judgment (10:5 ff.). When pitted against Yahweh's plan, any rival plan—whether Judah's political machinations (29:15-16; 30:1 ff.), or Assyria's haughty intentions (10:7 ff., 13-14), or any other nation's contrary purpose (7:5 ff.; 8:9-10; 19:1 ff.) —was doomed to utter failure. The "marvellous" plan of Yahweh would invalidate any human wisdom or counsel that failed to consider Yahweh. But for Isaiah, judgment was not the last word since Yahweh's plan ultimately entailed salvation for the people of God. Here three main concepts were envisioned: the remnant, the preservation of Zion, and the hope of the messianic Ruler.

Fichtner's main interest was not to assess the relationship between Isaiah's use of the wisdom vocabulary (*yāʿaṣ/ʿēṣā*) and the wise man's, although this was not left entirely out of view. Although I agree in the main with Fichtner's conclusions, I think his presentation is deficient for a number of reasons. First, his interpretation of Yahweh's plan has a certain rigidity which the Isaianic texts simply do not allow. For example, he portrays the *Heilsplan* as an integral part of Yahweh's comprehensive plan. Yet Fichtner himself recognizes that Isaiah does not use the *ʿēṣā* terminology for salvation, but

---

[51] For what follows, see Fichtner, *Gottes Weisheit,* pp. 30 ff.

only for judgment.[52] So it is questionable to talk about one comprehensive plan, whose two sides are stamped with the words "judgment and salvation." Secondly, Fichtner failed to consider more carefully the formative and positive influence of the wisdom traditions on Isaiah's understanding of Yahweh's plan. Thirdly, he did not consider the particular factors in Isaiah's historical situation that motivated the prophet to appropriate technical wisdom language for his most basic formulation of Yahweh's plan. Finally—albeit coupled with the third reason—Fichtner did not inquire sufficiently into the prophet's intentions in using this kind of language. Why did Isaiah choose *wisdom* language? To put the whole matter in another way: one must interpret more precisely the continuities and discontinuities between Isaiah and his wisdom traditions in light of the historical and existential situation in which the prophet worked in eighth-century Jerusalem. As much as possible one must get back to the "whys" and the "hows" of Isaiah's appropriation and adaptation of his traditions.

Our term appears in the following passages: with the verb $yā'as$ (in various forms) —1:26; 3:3; 7:5; 8:10 (*'ûs*) ; 9:5; 14:24, 26, 27; 19:11, 12, 17; 23:8, 9; 32:7-8; with the noun *'ēṣā*—5:19; 8:10; 11:2; 14:26; 16:3; 19:3, 11, 17; 28:29; 29:15; 30:1. Since Isa. 16:3; 19:3, 11, 12, 17; 23:8, 9; and 32:7, 8 are considered by most commentators to be non-Isaianic, they will not receive any detailed examination. Moreover, since I have already examined some of the key passages in other chapters (e.g., 14: 24-27; 28:23-29; 29:15-16) , it will be possible to deal with them in more summary form and to concentrate only on those elements that impinge particularly on our present problem.

A. ORACLES AGAINST JUDAH

1. Isa. 5:18-19

> Woe to those who draw iniquity with cords of falsehood,
>   who draw sin as with cart ropes,
> who say: "Let him make haste,

[52] *Ibid.,* p. 43.

> let him speed his work
> that we may see it;
> let the counsel of the Holy One of Israel draw near,
> and let it come, that we may know it!"

This passage contains one of the earliest references to the counsel of Yahweh. The speech follows a fairly typical pattern. Following the opening woe come the plural participles which describe the reprehensible behavior of those on whom the woe is pronounced.[53] They are characterized by both their deeds and words. It is the quotation of their words that is of particular importance for us, since it contains the reference to the "counsel (*'äṣat*) of the Holy One of Israel." The unidentified speakers apparently pick up key elements of Isaiah's message and mockingly hurl them back into his face. With scoffing tones, they call upon Yahweh to "hurry up" and get on with whatever he is going to do—which is expressed by the key terms "work" (*ma'ăśêh*) and "counsel" (*'ēṣā*). The first term seems to come out of cultic speech[54] and referred originally to Yahweh's work in creation[55] or in Israel's salvation history.[56] In contrast to the cultic usage, Isaiah means a completely new divine event which lies in the imminent future and which will bring an extreme crisis in its wake. The term is found elsewhere in Isaiah and seems to refer to the whole scope of

---

[53] See above Chapter III, "Woe Oracles and Wisdom."

[54] G. von Rad, "Das Werk Jahwes," *Studia Biblica et Semitica,* eds. W. C. van Unnik and A. S. van der Woude (Wageningen: H. Veenman, 1966) , pp. 290-98.

[55] H. Wildberger, "Jesajas Verständnis der Geschichte," VTS 9 (1962) : 95 ff. Note his conclusion: "Er [i.e., Isaiah] hat die erwartete Geschichte seines Gottes in Analogie zu Jahwes Schöpfungswerk verstanden. Der universale Herr der Schöpfung ist ihm zum universalen Herrn der Geschichte geworden" (p. 97) .

[56] So von Rad in opposition to Wildberger ("Das Werk Jahwes," pp. 295 ff.) . It is interesting to note in passing how von Rad has changed his view on the traditional roots of *ma'ăśêh*. In his *Old Testament Theology* II: 161, he says: "This concept of a 'work' of Jahweh can scarcely originate in a sacral tradition; it really looks like an independent coinage of Isaiah himself." In his more recent article, however, he shows convincingly that Isaiah is dependent on cultic tradition. Similarly, I feel von Rad is wrong to say that the concept of Yahweh's "counsel" (*'ēṣā*) is an Isaianic creation.

Yahweh's activity with Israel, whether in judgment (cf. 28:21) or in salvation (10:12). In our immediate context, it stands in synonymous parallelism with "counsel" and refers especially to Yahweh's counsel of judgment. The combination of the term "counsel" with "the Holy One of Israel" appears to be distinctively Isaianic, though the prophet had in his wisdom tradition the notion of a divine counsel. One interesting thing is that we find the juxtaposition of two terms that have diverse provenances—cultic and wisdom—and yet function more or less synonymously in the present context. This juxtaposition is uniquely Isaianic and illustrates the freedom with which Isaiah handled his traditional materials.

2. Isa. 29:15-16

> Woe to those who hide deep from Yahweh their counsel,
>> whose acts are in the dark,
>> and who say, "Who sees us? Who knows us?"
> O your perversity!
> Is the potter regarded as the clay?
> Can something made say of its maker,
>> "He did not make me"?
> or something fashioned say of its fashioner,
>> "He has no sense"?

Here the prophet does not mention Yahweh's counsel, but refers to the counsel of men. The oracle apparently stems from the last period of Isaiah's career and involves the feverish activities in Jerusalem court circles prior to the Assyrian crisis of 701 B.C. One must understand this historical background if he is to understand the oracle. In this crucial period Isaiah contested the politics that emanated from the Jerusalem court. The wise men in the court—the counsellors—wielded great influence in matters of state policy. It seems to have been the basic policy to avert the Assyrian peril by means of foreign alliances instead of reliance on Yahweh and trust in his plan (Isa. 30:1 ff.; 28:14 ff.; 31:1 ff.). To Isaiah this reflected a serious crisis within the wisdom circles and within the nation. In fact, the court wise men were illustrative of the dire straits of the whole nation, for they had forgotten a constituent feature of wisdom—the recognition of the limitations of human counsel over against Yahweh's. On the contrary, they had attempted to exceed the limits imposed on them by the fundamental fact of Yahweh's sovereignty. In his attack on the allegedly wise counsellors of the court, Isaiah draws upon their own traditions. From the perspective of the whole situation, the most effective way to counter the apostasy of the wise men was to meet them on common ground and condemn them with their own traditions.

Our present oracle graphically tells the tale. The passage consists of a woe invective, in which the prophet describes the deeds and words of the addressees in plural participles, adds a pejorative comment in the second person plural, and then concludes with a typical wisdom saying that highlights the tragic irony of the situation. The force of the reproach is patently and painfully clear: the wise men had disregarded the basic order of the world—that very order which was one of their fundamental presuppositions. Indeed, they had attempted to do the impossible—to hide their activity from the Creator. Their thinking was twisted and topsy-turvy, for they had tried to reverse positions with the Creator.[57] The awful irony of the situation was that they knew better! Isaiah's basic intention in using the terminology of wisdom here was a negative one: to refute as forcefully as possible the folly of the court wise men, Isaiah turns against them their *own* wisdom traditions.

Although it is a separate oracle, the immediately preceding speech serves as a commentary on 29:15-16. It sums up the divine judgment that will fall on Judah's wise men: "Behold, I will again do marvellous things with this people, wonderful and marvellous; and the wisdom of their wise men shall perish, and the discernment of their discerning men shall be hid" (Isa. 29:14). Yahweh's plan is marvellous (*pele'*) and will initiate something unexpected and uncanny. It will nullify the wise men's counsel which they have vainly tried to hide from Yahweh.

[57] See the analysis of the function of the wisdom saying (vs. 16) in Chapter II.

3. Isa. 30:1-5

"Woe to the rebellious children," says Yahweh
　"who carry out a counsel (*'ēṣā*), but not mine;
and who make a league, but not of my spirit,
　that they may add sin to sin;
who set out to go down to Egypt,
　without asking for my advice (*pî*)
to take refuge in the protection of Pharaoh,
　and to seek shelter in the shadow of Egypt!
Therefore shall the protection of Pharaoh turn to your
　　shame,
　and the shelter in the shadow of Egypt to your humiliation.
For though his officials are at Zóan and his envoys
　　reach Hánes,
every one comes to shame
　through a people that cannot profit them,
　that brings neither help nor profit, but shame and disgrace."

Whereas Isa. 29:15-16 talks about the counsel of the court
politicians in general terms, Isa. 30:1 ff. presents the specific
details of that counsel: a political treaty with Egypt. The
speech itself is a Yahweh oracle, which follows a typical pattern
of the invective-threat. As we saw in an earlier chapter, the
woe form has been altered by the particular concerns of the
historical hour. The woe contains the designation of the addressees as well as the motivation for judgment. The announcement of judgment comes in vss. 3-5 and consists essentially of
an ironic reversal of the intention of the people's plan: instead
of protection and shelter there will be shame and humiliation.
This passage contains in sharpest form the conflict between
Judah's counsel and Yahweh's. The folly of the people's action
was highlighted in Isa. 29:15-16; the certain failure of their
counsel is portrayed in the present passage.

4. Isa. 31:1-3

Woe to those who go down to Egypt for help
　and rely on horses,
who trust in chariots because they are many
　and in horsemen because they are very strong,
but do not look to the Holy One of Israel
　or consult Yahweh!

> And yet he is wise and brings disaster,
> he does not call back his words,
> but will arise against the house of the evildoers,
> and against the helpers of those who work iniquity.
> The Egyptians are men, and not God;
> and their horses are flesh, and not spirit.
> When Yahweh stretches out his hand
> the helper will stumble, and he who is helped will fall,
> and they will all perish together.

Although this passage does not contain 'ēṣā, the fact that it is a close parallel in content and form to Isa. 30:1 ff. shows that it moves in the same circle. Also, there is the explicit reference to Yahweh's wisdom which stands in contradiction to Judah's plan. Hence the passage has important implications for our topic.

The passage contains the now familiar woe invective which is followed by the announcement of judgment. Again, the motivation for judgment is Judah's trust in Egyptian military power and conversely her failure to look to Yahweh and consult him for his plan (vs. 1).[58] The announcement of judgment is given in general terms in vs. 2 and then in more specific terms in vs. 3. In the latter the rationale for judgment is again presented—this time by means of a comparison between God and the Egyptians (vs. 3a). The oracle concludes with the announcement of judgment for both the Egyptians and the Judeans: helper and helped alike will be destroyed. To Isaiah, only disaster can follow when Israel relies on man and not God.

Despite the deceptively simple cast of the oracle, it has some intrinsic difficulties to which B. S. Childs has called attention.[59] Vs. 2 constitutes the basic problem. Is it primary or secondary? To Childs it is the latter for a number of reasons.

[58] דרש is to consult the deity for advice, either directly (e.g., Gen. 25:22; II Kings 1:2, 3, 6, 16; Isa. 8:19; etc.) or more often through a mediator such as a prophet (e.g., I Kings 14:5; 22:5; II Kings 3:11; 8:8). Here the prophet adapts an old tradition, applying it to the political realm. This tradition has cultic roots and shows how the prophet weaves together different strands of tradition in his oracles.
[59] Childs, *Isaiah and the Assyrian Crisis*, pp. 34-35.

(1) The "almost reflective style [of vs. 2] fits poorly in an invective." (2) "Vs. 2 anticipates the striking contrast in vs. 3 of the Egyptians and God, while repeating in prosaic fashion the comprehensive character of the judgment." (3) Vs. 2 interrupts the correspondence between vss. 1 and 3. (4) The vocabulary of vs. 2, especially the vague, stereotyped description of the enemy, argues against the originality. (5) The close parallel between 30:1-5 and 31:1-3—except for 31:2— would seem to support the theory that 31:2 has been interpolated.

It must be admitted that Childs has assembled an impressive list of arguments which are telling in their cumulative effect. However, in assessing the weight of the data, he has failed to consider one highly important fact: the crucial element of the historical and existential situation which evoked such an oracle. I speak particularly of the crisis in court wisdom, which was of great importance to Isaiah. Childs seems to minimize this factor when he says with reference to vs. 2: "The sudden shift away from the contrast of the Egyptians with Yahweh to defend Yahweh's wisdom and power appears to belabour that which is otherwise assumed. . . ." [60] But Yahweh's wisdom and power were not assumed as a matter of course in Isaiah's situation; rather they were held in doubt in the ruling circles of the Jerusalem court, especially by the royal wise men. So the defense of Yahweh's wisdom was a prime concern to Isaiah. Once again we may cite the quotations which Isaiah places in the mouths of his opponents:

> "Let him make haste, let him speed his work that we may see it;
> let the counsel of the Holy One of Israel draw near,
> and let it come, that we may know it!" (Isa. 5:19)

> Woe to those who hide deep from Yahweh their counsel,
> whose acts are in the dark,
> and who say, "Who sees us? Who knows us?" (Isa. 29:15)

We may add to these statements the Parable of the Farmer (Isa. 28:23 ff.) which explicitly defends Yahweh's wisdom and

[60] *Ibid.*, p. 34.

counsel. All these data, most of which stem from the same historical period as 31:1 ff., would seem to make questionable the theory of interpolation which Childs proposes. To the allegations that Yahweh's wisdom was suspect, Isaiah could answer with biting irony: Yahweh "too is wise and brings disaster" (31:2a). Since Yahweh's wisdom was under fire, Isaiah was compelled by the needs of the historical hour to defend Yahweh's wisdom—even if this meant "to belabour that which is otherwise assumed." [61] Therefore I should argue that the nature of Isaiah's historical situation makes it highly probable that 31:2 is an original part of the oracle—at least one should be more cautious about relegating it to the category of a later interpolation. Here again it would appear that the historical factors have altered the invective-threat pattern of the oracle and made it more complex, thus accounting in part for the difficulties that Childs points out. In my judgment, the evidence indicates that the oracle is another illustration of why the full understanding of Isaiah's historical and existential situation is an indispensable prerequisite for interpreting the complexities of his oracles.

B. ORACLES AGAINST THE NATIONS

Here I shall deal principally with the two main oracles that concern Assyria's role in Yahweh's counsel and plan: Isa. 14: 24-27 and Isa. 10:5-15. For our purposes there is no need to treat at length Isa. 7:5 ff. and 8:9-10, except to say that both give expression to Yahweh's nullification of the plans of foreign nations.[62] Again, they highlight Isaiah's typically sharp contrast between Yahweh's plan and the opposing plans of men.

We may also mention in passing such secondary passages as Isa. 19:11, 12, 17 and 23:8, 9. For example, we read:

The princes of Zóan are utterly foolish;
    the wise counsellors of Pharaoh give stupid counsel ('ēṣā).

[61] *Ibid.*
[62] On Isa. 8:9, 10, see the exegesis of M. Saebö, "Zur Traditionsgeschichte von Jesaia 8:9-10," ZAW 76 (1964) : 132 ff., esp. p. 137.

How can you say to Pharaoh,
"I am a son of the wise,
a son of ancient kings"?
Where then are your wise men?
Let them tell you and make known
what Yahweh has decided (yā'aṣ) against Egypt. (Isa. 19:11, 12)

This passage embodies clear-cut wisdom elements, albeit in distinctively prophetic fashion (a mocking speech). It shows the continued life of the motif of Yahweh's counsel versus man's in the post-Isaianic traditions; the influence of Isaiah on his successors is surely apparent. One could say the same about the oracle against Tyre in Isa. 23:8, 9, where the concept of Yahweh's counsel again comes to the fore.

1. Isa. 14:24-27

Yahweh of hosts has sworn:
"As I have purposed, so shall it be,
    and as I have decided (yā'āṣtî), so shall it stand,
that I will break the Assyrian in my land,
    and upon my mountains trample him under foot;
    and his yoke shall depart from them,
    and his burden from their shoulder."
This is the counsel (hā'ēṣā) that is decided (hayyeʿûṣā)
    concerning the whole earth;
and this is the hand that is stretched out
    over all the nations.
For Yahweh of hosts has decided (yā'aṣ)
    and who will annul it?
His hand is stretched out,
    and who will turn it back?

Since we have already dealt form critically with this passage, it will be necessary only to draw out the implications for our present topic. As we noted previously the passage combines a Yahweh speech (vss. 24-25) with a kind of prophetic commentary (vss. 26-27). The former is a threat introduced by an oath formula, and the latter a "summary-appraisal form" (vs. 26) [63] which is then grounded by two parallel assertions,

[63] Childs, *Isaiah and the Assyrian Crisis*, pp. 128 ff.; see also my treatment of this form in Chapter II.

each with a rhetorical question (vs. 27). The technical wisdom language (yā'aṣ, 'ēṣā) plus the wisdom form (the summary-appraisal) indicates an integral part of the traditionary background on which Isaiah is drawing. What is striking is the fusion of the divine speech in the I-form with the prophet's wisdom reflection.

The theme of Yahweh's counsel or plan is the glue that holds the passage together in a cohesive unity. Nowhere else in his oracles does Isaiah speak so fully and precisely about Yahweh's counsel; so the passage is decisive for clarifying the character and function of Yahweh's counsel in Isaiah.

In the present context, the central thrust of Yahweh's counsel is the decision to destroy Assyria. Isaiah, however, is careful to emphasize that Assyria's destiny is but a part of a comprehensive plan embracing the whole earth (vs. 26). This plan will be materialized in a disaster that will overtake Assyria. In the announcement of Assyria's ultimate doom, Judah's destiny is not completely left out of view. A reflex of Assyria's demise will be Judah's deliverance. An indirect promise of deliverance is found in vs. 25b: "His yoke shall depart from them, and his burden from their shoulder."

In this text Yahweh is portrayed as the Master Counsellor, whose counsel stretches over the expanse of world history and is utterly effective. In the context of the crisis in wisdom, the contrast between Yahweh as the Master Counsellor and the court wise men—whether in Israel or in the nations—cannot fail to be noted. In this regard it is interesting that Isaiah borrows a wisdom form (vs. 26) to emphasize the nature of Yahweh's counsel. One surely is not misreading the data to say that Isaiah is radically opposing Yahweh's counsel to any and all contrary plans. This implicit polemical [64] thrust of the passage would seem to be confirmed in the concluding rhetorical questions: "For Yahweh of hosts has decided, and who will annul it? His hand is stretched out, and who will turn it back?" (vs. 27). Can one not hear in these assertions and ques-

[64] Isaiah's polemical intention in appropriating wisdom language is well brought out by McKane, pp. 66 ff.

tions a defiant challenge which Isaiah hurls against all those who are ostensibly wise and yet have attempted to formulate contrary plans? The echo of a passage like Prov. 19:21 cannot be missed: "Many are the plans in the mind of man, but it is the counsel of Yahweh that will be established." But one should not miss the contrast between the prophetic and wisdom contexts: whereas the prophet fills the concept of Yahweh's counsel with a *specific* content, the wise man typically expresses a *generalization* drawn from his experience and observation of the interplay between the divine and human counsels. Both prophet and wise man, however, unite in affirming that when Yahweh's counsel is pitted against man's there is no contest—Yahweh's will always comes out on top.

2. Isa. 10:5-15 [65]

Although form critical criteria militate against the popular thesis of Cheyne that 14:24-27 is the original conclusion to 10:5-15,[66] the two passages nevertheless reflect the same Isaianic concerns and seems to belong in the same historical and theological context. Yahweh's counsel is the fundamental coordinate that binds the two passages together in theme and theology. To be sure, there are different emphases. In 14:24-27 the accent is on Yahweh's utterly effective design for Assyria's destruction, whereas Isa. 10:5 ff. presents the grounds for Assyria's doom. In our more detailed exegesis of the latter passage, we observed the skillful way Isaiah nakedly unveils the folly and culpability of Assyria. What is important for our immediate purposes is that the passage shows the impact of the theological concept of Yahweh's counsel.[67] The sharp conflict between Yahweh's plan and Assyria's could not be more forcefully drawn. Isaiah stresses the utter futility of Assyria's high-handed activity. No nation can stop the actualization of Yahweh's counsel, and woe betide the nation that tries (cf. also Isa. 7:5 ff.; 8:10). The wisdom saying in vs. 15 epitomizes

---

[65] For a more detailed exegesis of this passage, see Chapter II.
[66] Childs, *Isaiah and the Assyrian Crisis,* p. 38.
[67] Childs makes this same emphasis (*ibid.,* p. 44).

the folly of Assyria's activity as well as Isaiah's confident recognition of the futility of Assyria's opposition to Yahweh's plan.

C. ORACLES OF PROMISE

In this section we move to dimensions of the counsel/counsellor motif that are different from what we have been considering. Whereas the previous passages involved either Yahweh's plan of judgment or the contrary plans of men, the next oracles we will consider deal with the institution of counsellor (Isa. 1:26) and the expertise in counsel that will characterize the Messiah (Isa. 9:5; Isa. 11:2). Again, our main interest is to see how Isaiah reflects influence from the wisdom traditions and how he adapts these traditions in light of his own concerns.

1. Isa. 1:26

". . . I will restore your judges as at the first,
    and your counselors as at the beginning.
Afterward you shall be called the city of righteousness,
    the faithful city."

This passage is the last part of a complex oracle (1:21-26) which embraces a number of disparate formal elements. A structural analysis shows the matter clearly:

I. Prophetic Speech: Invective in the Form of a Lament (vss. 21-23)
II. Yahweh Speech (vss. 24-26)
   A. Introduction: Messenger Formula (vs. 24a)
   B. Announcement of Purificatory Judgment (vss. 24b-25)
   C. Promise of Restoration (vs. 26)

Despite the diversity of speech forms, a careful look at the speech shows that the prophet has woven the elements together into an artistic unity. The speech is marked by chiastic symmetry (cf. the correspondence between 21a and 26b, 21b and 26a, 22 and 25, 23 and 24b).[68] This structural feature alone demonstrates that the speech is a unity. One of the interesting things about the speech is how judgment and salva-

[68] Cf. Fey, *Amos und Jesaja*, pp. 64 ff.

tion are fused together into an organic unity. The restoration is envisaged as standing at the end of the process of a purifying judgment. So the very structure of the speech corresponds to the pattern of judgment and salvation.

What is significant for our interests is the reference to the "counsellors" (vs. 26a) who will play a signal role in the Jerusalem of the future. It is clear that Isaiah is depending on his Jerusalemite-Davidic traditions. The phrases "at the first"//"at the beginning" can only refer here to the Davidic period which was Jerusalem's heyday. Following a historicized *Urzeit-Endzeit* pattern comes Isaiah's declaration that the future of Jerusalem will be modeled on the past. And the counsellors will be a fundamental part of the new society. Although Isaiah pronounced a harsh sentence on the *present* counsellors and wise men (Isa. 29:14, 15-16; 3:3), this does not mean he condemned the institution of counsellors per se. There was a time, at the beginning, when the counsellors were front-ranking members of the "City of righteousness." Along with the judges, the counsellors are prototypical images of the leadership that Jerusalem once had. As leading lights in Jerusalemite officialdom, they had a key role in the maintenance of communal solidarity—the righteousness of Jerusalem.

In light of Isaiah's existential situation where he was pitted so often against the counsellors of the Jerusalem court, it is not overinterpreting the passage to hear an indirect rebuke of his contemporaries in his emphasis that Yahweh will "restore the counsellors *as at the beginning.*" The pattern for the restoration would not be the contemporary counsellors, but rather their predecessors from the ideal past, who were loyal to Yahweh and worthy representatives of wisdom. Of course this is not to overlook the role of tradition as a primary force in shaping Isaiah's vision of the future. But the traditional factor does not enable us to sidestep the question of how his existential situation has influenced his use of the materials.

In conclusion, it is evident that Isaiah's view of the institution of counsellor was not a simplistic black and white (as McKane would argue) but a complex portrait. So Isaiah condemned his contemporary counsellors, but not the institution per se. For when he wanted to portray the restoration he envisioned the royal *"counsellors"* as an integral part of the Jerusalem of the future.

2. Isa. 11:1-5 and Isa. 9:5*b*[69]

It has long been recognized that Isaiah relies heavily on wisdom traditions in his portrait of the coming Messiah. In Isa. 11:1 ff. the wisdom influence particularly comes to the fore, and in Isa. 9:5*b* one of the Messiah's throne names is "wonder of a counsellor." In Isa. 11:1 ff., Isaiah utilizes a whole spate of wisdom terms to describe the character of the coming Ruler:

> And the Spirit of Yahweh will rest upon him,
> the spirit of wisdom and understanding,
> the spirit of counsel and might,
> the spirit of knowledge and the fear of Yahweh.
> (Isa. 11:2)

This wisdom is particularly linked with the judicial responsibility (Isa. 11:4-5). The traditionary roots of this kind of wisdom are sunk deeply in the soil of the ancient Near East and such royal wisdom was used to describe both David and Solomon.[70] For example, the wise woman of Tekoa once said of David: ". . . my lord has wisdom like the wisdom of the angel of God to know all things that are on the earth" (II Sam. 14:20). Solomon's wisdom is described even more extravagantly (cf. I Kings 3:5 ff.; 4:29 ff.). One of the two basic types of wisdom that tradition accords to Solomon is judicial wisdom, by which he was able to rule his people justly (cf. I Kings 3:9, 29).[71] There is no doubt, then, as to the type of wisdom traditions Isaiah was drawing on.

[69] It is still an open question whether these oracles belong to the eighth-century Isaiah. However, an emerging consensus would argue for their Isaianic vintage. For the most recent treatment of the whole problem of salvation promises in prophecy, cf. S. Herrmann, *Die prophetischen Heilserwartungen im Alten Testament* (Stuttgart: W. Kohlhammer, 1965), pp. 130 ff.

[70] Cf. N. W. Porteous, "Royal Wisdom," VTS 3 (1955) : 247 ff.

[71] Cf. A. Alt, "Die Weisheit Salomos," ThLZ 76 (1951) : 139-44.

In the case of Isa. 9:5*b*, the name "wonder of a counsellor" is a part of a royal titulary whose original roots lie in Egypt.[72] To be sure, Isaiah has put his special stamp on it. Against the whole backdrop of Isaiah's message where there is so much emphasis on "counsel," it is significant that he gives such a title to the Messiah. For example, one certainly hears the echo of the characterization of Yahweh as one who is "wonderful in counsel" (*hiplî 'ēṣā*, Isa. 28:29*b*).

What is particularly significant for our purpose is how Isaiah uses the counsel/counsellor motif. Again, it is necessary to set the passages against the historical backdrop in order to perceive why and how Isaiah adapts this specific wisdom term. We have observed that Isaiah perceived a crisis in court wisdom. The royal wise men had compromised their traditions and perpetrated a counterfeit version. They had disregarded the divine limits and attempted to go on alone with no consideration of Yahweh's purpose. Isaiah attacked the wise men at this point, reactualizing and radicalizing their own traditions in order to do it.

It is within the context of this crisis that one must understand Isaiah's portrayal of the Messiah. In contrast to the rebel wise men whose counsel was in deep contradiction to Yahweh's, the Messiah would be a "wonder of a counsellor" (9:5*b*) who would be in harmony with Yahweh's will. The use of the root *pl'* impressively attests the Messiah's superiority over the contemporary royal counsellors.[73] Moreover, the Messiah would receive Yahweh's spirit and a set of charismatic gifts, which centered fundamentally in a wisdom that would enable him to execute judicial functions. This is one of the functions that had fallen into disrepair in the contemporary ruling circles at the Jerusalem court (cf. Isa. 1:23; 10:1, 2; etc.). In contrast, the coming Messiah would perform perfectly the judicial responsibilities laid upon the Davidic ruler. One of these gifts of Yahweh's spirit is "counsel and might." This duo seems to be a

[72] For a good summary of the evidence, see Herrmann, pp. 135 ff.; also H. Wildberger, "Die Thronnamen des Messias, Jes. 9:5*b*," TZ 76 (1960): 316 and 329 ff.

[73] Wildberger, "Die Thronnamen des Messias, Jes. 9:5*b*," p. 316.

stereotyped phrase, which is used of both man (II Kings 18: 20//Isa. 36:5) and God (Job 12:13). It highlights the fact that the authority and power of a counsellor are decisively important: one must be able to effect the counsel he has formulated. The Messiah has this power to the highest degree. The secret of his success is his "fear of Yahweh" which is the foundation of Israelite wisdom.

D. THE PARABLES OF THE FARMER (ISA. 28:23-29)

We have already done a full exegesis of this passage[74] and need only to summarize the implications it has for our present question. Although it is the last passage with which we shall deal, it is one of the most important. First of all, it offers compelling evidence for the wisdom provenance of the technical term "counsel"—and in particular of Yahweh's counsel, for its speech forms and traditions are patently wisdom in origin. Secondly, it gives valuable insight into how Isaiah appropriated the wisdom tradition as one way to wrestle with the problem of Yahweh's activity in history. As von Rad puts it: "Written evidence of this expressly rational grappling with history is furnished by . . . the didactic poem in Is. xxviii. 23-29, in which Isaiah makes the multifarious and carefully considered actions of the farmer's sowing and reaping into a transparent parable of the divine action in history." [75]

The parable functions as a disputation: Isaiah answers the criticisms against Yahweh's seemingly haphazard and inconsistent activities. Just as the divinely taught farmer varies his agricultural labors according to different needs and times, so Yahweh varies his activities according to the demands of the historical situation. The climax of Isaiah's argument is reached in the concluding sentence: "He is wonderful in counsel and excellent in sound wisdom" (Isa. 28:29b). One of the striking features of the passage is the way Isaiah argues: just as the farmer in his agricultural labors manifests the character of the divine counsel, so the whole field of history becomes the arena

[74] See above Chapter II.
[75] G. von Rad, *Old Testament Theology* II: 184.

where Yahweh's counsel is materialized. Employing the familiar wisdom technique of forming analogies between seemingly disparate spheres,[76] Isaiah perceives a deep, underlying affinity between agriculture and history: both are fields in which Yahweh's wise counsel is decisively effective. By this means Isaiah is able to argue that Yahweh's seemingly haphazard activity has an inner consistency because it is governed by Yahweh's counsel and wisdom. In Isaiah's usage of the parable the oft repeated dictum that wisdom is timeless and unrelated to history is completely inapplicable.[77] On the contrary, Isaiah is able to adopt wisdom categories in order to reflect on the problem of Yahweh's activities in history: like the wise man, Yahweh matches the proper activity with the proper time. This passage is an illuminating and profound example of how Isaiah has creatively actualized his wisdom traditions for his own purposes.

IV. CONCLUDING OBSERVATIONS

First, my major conclusion is that in his usage of $yā'aṣ/'ēṣā$ Isaiah manifests strong influences from the wisdom traditions of the Jerusalem court which were both negative and positive in their effects. The negative impact is revealed in Isaiah's clashes with the court wise men. He envisaged the powerful influence exerted by the political wise men as a threat to Yahwistic faith and condemned the wise in no uncertain terms (29:14b, 15-16; 31:1 ff.). Moreover, Isaiah was able to condemn the wise men according to their own ground rules, which they had either forgotten or ignored. Their own traditions should have been sufficient warning that Yahweh's counsel always prevailed over man's (cf. Gen. 50:20; Prov. 19: 21; 20:30, 31).

But the influence was also positive. Isaiah appropriated the concept of Yahweh's counsel or plan from wisdom circles and applied it to Yahweh's activities within the present (and future) historical situation (cf. again Gen. 50:20 and Prov.

---

[76] Cf. von Rad, *Old Testament Theology* I: 424 ff.
[77] See the solid criticism of this dictum in Schmid, pp. 4 ff.

19:21 with Isa. 14:24-27; 28:29). This plan was being materialized particularly within the context of the contemporary
political events of the ancient Near East (Isa. 10:5 ff.; 14:
24 ff.). In this regard, Yahweh was a master counsellor, who
always executed his plan with the right method for the right
time (Isa. 28:23 ff.). Finally, no one could thwart Yahweh's
counsel, and disaster awaited the one who tried (Isa. 10:5 ff.;
14:24 ff.; 30:1 ff.; 31:1 ff.).

In still another dimension the wisdom traditions left a positive imprint on Isaiah's message: this was in his picture of the
future restoration. In one place, he announces that the institution of counsellors will be restored according to the pattern
of the Davidic era (1:26b). Also, he uses clear-cut wisdom elements to portray Yahweh's Messiah, who will be a "wonder
of a counsellor" (9:5b) and will receive the spirit of "counsel
and might" (11:2).

Secondly, the question of the possible influence from the
mythological background on the idea of Yahweh's 'ēṣā must be
left open.[78] That the concept of Yahweh's heavenly council
within which political decrees were decided left its imprint
on Isaiah's understanding of Yahweh's purpose is probable.
Isaiah's report of his vocation clearly demonstrates that this
mythological tradition was at the forefront of his thinking
(cf. I Kings 22 and Isa. 6). Also, the first part of Isa. 14:24-27
—whose fundamental theme is that of Yahweh's 'ēṣā—is given
in the form of an *Auditionsbericht,* which perhaps implies that
Isaiah was privy to the divine council. Finally, the concept of
Yahweh as King (6:5) possibly led Isaiah to see Yahweh in
analogy to the court circles, to which the notion of counsel
was intimately joined. This connection is especially suggestive when one thinks of the fact that wisdom was considered
the special prerogative of a king (cf. Isa. 9:5 and 11:2).[79]

The difficulty with von Rad's thesis is that the term 'ēṣā and

---

[78] G. von Rad, *Old Testament Theology* II: 162.

[79] After this chapter was completed I received the third fascicle of Wildberger's commentary on Isaiah in which he also argues for the intimate
connections between Yahweh's kingship and the wisdom usage of 'ēṣā
(*Jesaia,* p. 189).

the heavenly council are nowhere in the Old Testament explicitly linked. To be sure, this is no insurmountable obstacle and the analogy of the earthly king and his council where counsel is formulated is good support for von Rad's proposal. On the other side, we have shown the real resonance between Isaiah's use of 'ēṣā and the wise man's. This is supported by both internal and external evidence, which indicates that wisdom is the dominant traditionary background on which Isaiah drew. Both the express terminology ('āṣat yhwh, Prov. 19:21b) and the concept of Yahweh's plan (e.g., Gen. 50:20) are present in wisdom materials. Although especially adapted, Isaiah's basic terminology and conceptualization of Yahweh's 'ēṣā closely parallels the picture in early wisdom. Taken together the cumulative force of the evidence seems irrefutable.

Of course our view of the wisdom backdrop of Yahweh's 'ēṣā does not necessarily rule out other traditional influences like the mythological concept of the heavenly council. In fact, one could cautiously suggest that we have a confluence of the two backgrounds in Isaiah, united by the central concept of Yahweh as King who in his heavenly council formulates his counsel and plan. If this interpretation is reasonably accurate, it would have a number of implications for our study. First of all, it shows the interpenetration of mythological imagery from the cult and court wisdom. It is simply remiss to separate too rigidly between these two realms of Israelite life. Moreover, Isaiah, as we have seen time and time again, borrowed out of both backgrounds, combining the different traditions into new configurations. Against the royal background of the Jerusalem court and cult, Isaiah appropriated both sets of tradition. By this means, Isaiah authenticated himself as prophet both by claiming the reception of Yahweh's counsel in the heavenly council and by confronting the court wise men on their own ground, utilizing the concept of Yahweh's counsel drawn from their wisdom tradition. To Isaiah, there was a basic congruence between the divine counsel which he received in the heavenly council and the observable operation of that counsel in history. It is unwise therefore to distinguish sharply between what the prophet received in visionary revelation and what he, like the wise man, could observe in the realities of historical experience.

Thirdly, throughout this chapter we have asked why Isaiah used a *wisdom* term and concept. To answer this question we looked to Isaiah's historical situation in eighth-century Jerusalem. First of all, as a Jerusalemite, he had available to him all the wisdom traditions that were present at the royal court from the days of the Davidic-Solomonic era on. Also, there was a resurgence in interest in wisdom at the Jerusalem court in Isaiah's day—especially under King Hezekiah (cf. Prov. 25:1). So it is natural in one sense that Isaiah tapped the wisdom traditions as one source of material. However, one cannot stop here, for this is scarcely sufficient to answer our question; the simple fact that certain wisdom traditions were available does not explain why Isaiah used them. In my judgment, the answer lies in the nature of the extreme crisis Isaiah faced in his own historical situation. To Isaiah's eye the court wise men had played a leading role in fomenting the crisis, for they had advocated policies that were inimical to Yahwistic faith. Therefore, just as Hosea had daringly appropriated mythological terms and traditions from Canaanite religion in order to oppose the kind of apostasy he faced in the Northern Kingdom, so Isaiah had borrowed the vocabulary and traditions of wisdom in order to combat the apostasy engendered in part by the royal wise men. In other words, the nature of the situation helped shape the prophetic response. By using wisdom traditions—both to condemn the ostensibly wise and to defend the true Yahwistic wisdom—Isaiah was able to speak a pertinent message to the particular problems of his own situation. Until one sees this existential and historical backdrop, he will fail to understand fully Isaiah's adaptation of wisdom terminology.

Finally, it is necessary to say a word about the implications of Isaiah's use of ʿēṣā for his role as political advisor. As is evident, I have dealt with Isaiah's political involvement only as it relates to his employment of one technical wisdom term which springs out of the political context of court wisdom. I concentrated especially on an analysis of the particular functions of ʿēṣā in Isaiah's message in relationship to the traditional and contemporary backdrop of court wisdom. So I have purposely not entered into a discussion of the whole complex problem of the prophet and politics since this is a many-faceted question whose examination would require one to go far beyond the more limited objectives of the present study.[80] To be sure, my work does have implications for the larger problem and may shed a little light on some of the central issues.

My fundamental concern has been to show in a limited area something of the style and substance of Isaiah's reaction to the concrete political issues of his day. As we have seen, he felt both the freedom and the necessity to engage both king and court wise men in active dialogue on the question of whose counsel should be followed in specific political crises—Yahweh's or man's. This encounter is illustrative of Isaiah's stance on politics. Especially noteworthy is how he could engage his opponents on the same ground, appropriating their own terminology, traditions, and techniques in argument in order to demonstrate the futility and folly of their political advice. From the perspective of Yahweh's counsel or plan, Isaiah assessed the complex national and international political developments. To be sure, the notion of Yahweh's counsel does not become an abstract and absolute principle, but it is always seen in the context of particular issues. If there be any principle, it is that Yahweh's counsel will prevail over any and all counsels of man; before Yahweh's counsel the pride of the nations will be smashed (cf. Isa. 7:5; 8:9; 10:5-15; 14:24-27; 29:15-16; 30:1-5; 31:1-3). Also, in his own political outlook Isaiah was confident that Yahweh's counsel was marked by an inner cogency and consistency—despite the dark ambiguities of Yahweh's action in history (Isa. 28:23-29). As we have noted, it is wrong therefore to drive a sharp wedge between Isaiah's empirical evaluation of the political realities and his vision of the world vouchsafed in the heavenly council. In sum, Isaiah was able to combine in his political perspective—with no apparent tension—the wise man's empirical assessment and the prophet's vision.

[80] See Gottwald's perceptive summary and critique of the various alternatives proposed in the history of interpretation (pp. 347 ff.).

V

Conclusion

The basic purpose of this study was to examine the relationship between Isaiah and the wisdom traditions. Taking as a starting point J. Fichtner's suggestion of Isaiah's intimate connections with wisdom, I attempted to go beyond Fichtner's incomplete and inadequate treatment. The driving concern was therefore to do a more comprehensive analysis of the wisdom materials in Isaiah than had hitherto been done. I sought particularly to clarify and illumine the pertinent texts by a form critical analysis, trying to be sensitive to the nuances of Isaiah's use of wisdom traditions.

It is now appropriate to summarize the results of the study and to draw some conclusions. A synthesis of the results will highlight the cumulative effect of the case for wisdom influence on Isaianic preaching. First of all, the variety of wisdom genres analyzed in Chapter II is sufficient evidence to confirm the significant role of wisdom in Isaiah. So Isaiah employs two parables (1:3; 5:1-7) to indict Israel for her long history of apostasy. By correlating examples from agriculture and the animal kingdom with Israel's behavior, Isaiah can more forcefully condemn Israel for her apostasy, which is contrary to nature when viewed from the perspective of wisdom and is tantamount to a violation of the created order. Still another parable (Isa. 28:23-29) demonstrates the wisdom of Yahweh in his activities, employing the analogy of the farmer. It seems to have served as Isaiah's rejoinder to critics of Yahweh's wisdom; it is also an index to Isaiah's understanding of the consistency and wisdom of Yahweh's activities in the world. Moreover, the proverbial sayings (10:15 and 29:16) and summary-appraisals (14:26; 28:29) highlight Isaiah's use of wisdom speech. In particular, the "disputation-fables" in Isa. 10:15 and 29:16— coming at pivotal places in Isaiah's message—testify not simply to the mere use of proverbial language, but suggest a distinctive wisdom style of argumentation which Isaiah felt free to utilize when the context demanded it.

The analysis of woe speeches in Chapter III showed not only the appropriation of what is probably an old wisdom genre, but indicated on the basis of the content the essential relatedness of wisdom and law. It is therefore risky to over-stress Isaiah's function as a preacher of "law," for the sources of his ethical concepts are more complex than that formulation allows. Such a formulation suggests a rigidity and abstraction in the whole concept of law which the data do not admit and fails to give due heed to the popular ethos as a source on which Isaiah (and other prophets) can draw for the indictment of social injustice. By saying this I do not mean to rule the legal traditions out of the picture, but only to suggest that there are wide overlaps between law and wisdom in Israel. As Gerstenberger has convincingly demonstrated, both law and wisdom go back to common roots in the "clan ethos" (*Sippenethos*).[1] To set law over against wisdom as a superior source of ethical norms because of some concept of a divinely revealed Israelite law is erroneous and ignores the similar substance and hence common origins of law and wisdom in the popular ethos. One needs therefore to exercise extreme care when talking about "law" in the prophets, lest he fall into the error of positing an abstract view of Israelite law (on which the prophets are supposed to be dependent) which is both distinct from and superior to the age-old ethical rules of the popular ethos.

A particular wisdom term—"counsel" ('*ēṣā*) —was the pri-

---

[1] Gerstenberger, *Wesen und Herkunft des "apodiktischen Rechts,"* pp. 110 ff.; *idem*, "Woe-Oracles," p. 264.

mary focus of Chapter IV, for it concerned a central theme of Isaiah. The basic thesis was that Isaiah did not invent the concept of Yahweh's counsel but rather appropriated it from wisdom circles, though he transformed it and filled it with his own distinctive content. The term is therefore decisive in demonstrating another dimension of wisdom influence on Isaiah. It is especially important because it shows the contours of Isaiah's encounter with the wisdom circles of the Jerusalem court. On the one hand, he borrowed a key term and concept from their wisdom traditions; and on the other, he used that concept against the court wise men and condemned them for opposing their own counsel against Yahweh's—an act that was both foolish and fatal.

Certain broader conclusions flow from the basic results of our examination of wisdom in Isaiah. First, we may assert that our study confirms Fichtner's original thesis of a vital connection between Isaiah and wisdom, though we demur with respect to Fichtner's explanation of Isaiah as a former wise man become prophet. Moreover, our study cited additional evidence of wisdom influence on Isaiah which Fichtner either overlooked or inadequately treated (e.g., new forms like the summary-appraisal and the woe indictment, new thematic connections of wisdom and law, and new insight into the wisdom background of integral Isaianic motifs like Yahweh's counsel). Finally, in a more detailed exegesis of the pertinent data we attempted to go beyond Fichtner in the question of the "hows" and "whys" behind Isaiah's utilization of wisdom materials—something which in our judgment Fichtner failed to do.

Secondly, wisdom influence appears in Isaiah at different levels. It can show up in Isaiah as a way of speaking which if not directly borrowed from wisdom at least finds its best analogy in wisdom speech (e.g., the popular proverbs like 10:15 and 29:16). Here one must discriminate as much as possible between popular wisdom and more technical wisdom. So the use of proverbs or even parables does not necessarily prove a direct borrowing from a particular wisdom school which transmitted such materials. Such genres could simply be taken from popular speech. However, in light of the resurgence of the wisdom movement in the eighth century (especially in Hezekiah's reign, cf. Prov. 25:1), and in light of Isaiah's explicit contacts and conflicts with court wise men, the motivation for the usage of wisdom speech—whether popular or technical—seems likely to stem from Isaiah's connections with wisdom circles at the Jerusalem court. Though of course this cannot be absolutely proven, the probabilities seem clearly to favor such a reading of the data. I should argue then that in part at least Isaiah's historical and existential context in Jerusalem was instrumental in motivating Isaiah to use a plethora of wisdom materials. To him the utilization of wisdom speech was one of the ways to meet head on the problems of eighth-century Judah. By stylizing his preaching according to wisdom patterns —one of the most influential ways of speech at the Jerusalem court—and by appropriating wisdom terms and themes for his preaching, Isaiah could more effectively speak to the situation that confronted him. So I should conclude that the high incidence of wisdom materials in Isaiah points to the intellectual climate of his eighth-century Jerusalem context. It shows how time and again a prophet creatively stylized his message according to the demands of his own day and how a particular context helped to shape the prophetic response.

Finally, the study highlights the artificiality of the oft-drawn contrast between prophetic insight gained by his empirical observation (à la the wise man) and that given in visionary form. One must raise the question whether such a distinction is basically modern and is inappropriate to the data. To be sure, on the descriptive level one can clearly point out the differences when the prophet uses language that refers to a visionary experience (e.g., the call narrative in Isa. 6) in contrast to language that reflects a wisdom approach based on empirical observation and argumentation (e.g., the parable of the farmer in Isa. 28:23 ff.). On the substantive level, however, it is unwise to press for the priority or superiority of one type of language and the understanding of reality contained in it over against another type. It seems dubious that the prophet would consider any less true his understanding of

Yahweh as a God who acts with unerring wisdom (Isa. 28: 23 ff.) as compared with his vision of Yahweh's glory and holiness as the King of the universe (Isa. 6). In brief, the different kinds of language do not argue for the greater authenticity of one over against the other. In a world dominated by Yahweh, it seems accurate to say that the prophet would see a basic consistency and unity in the knowledge he gained by empirical observation and that given to him in visionary experience. I say this against the position that has a restricted view of the prophet as one whose message is to be interpreted only in categories of visionary or supernaturally revealed "truths." It is this type of position which argues against the authenticity of certain wisdom materials in the prophets on the basis that a wisdom style of speaking did not jibe with a genuinely "prophetic" posture. In short, it is inappropriate to place value judgments on the different approaches of the prophet to reality and to assert that one approach is superior to another.

Bibliography

Alt, A. *Essays on Old Testament History and Religion.* Trans. R. A. Wilson. New York: Doubleday & Co., 1967.

————. "Die Weisheit Salomos," ThLZ 76 (1951) : 139-44.

Anderson, R. T. "Was Isaiah a Scribe?" JBL 79 (1960) : 57-58.

Anthes, R. *Lebensregeln und Lebensweisheit der alten Ägypter.* "Der alte Orient," 32/2. Leipzig: J. C. Hinrichs, 1933.

Audet, J. P. "Origines comparées de la double tradition de la loi et la sagesse dans la proche-orient ancien," *International Congress of Orientalists* (25th). Moscow (1960), I: 352-57.

Bach, R. "Gottesrecht und weltliches Recht in der Verkündigung des Propheten Amos," *Festschrift Günther Dehn.* Neukirchen: Neukirchener Verlag (1957), pp. 23-34.

Baltzer, K. *Das Bundesformular.* WMANT, Band 4. Neukirchen-Vlyun: Neukirchener Verlag, 1960.

Baumgartner, W. "Die israelitische Weisheitsliteratur," ThR NF 5 (1933) : 259-88.

————. "The Wisdom Literature," *The Old Testament and Modern Study.* Ed. H. H. Rowley. Oxford: The Clarendon Press, 1952.

Becker, J. *Gottesfurcht im Alten Testament.* "Analecta Biblica," 25. Rome: Pontifical Biblical Institute, 1965.

Begrich, J. *Gesammelte Studien zum Alten Testament.* "Theologische Bücherei, "Band 21. München: Chr. Kaiser Verlag, 1964.

————. "Sōfer und Mazkīr. Ein Beitrag zur inneren Geschichte des davidisch-salomonischen Grossreiches und des Königreiches Juda," ZAW 58 (1940/41) : 1-29.

————. *Studien zu Deuterojesaja.* "Theologische Bücherei," Band 20. München: Chr. Kaiser Verlag, 1963.

Bentzen, A. *Introduction to the Old Testament,* I and II. 6th ed. Copenhagen: G. E. C. Gad Publisher, 1961.

————. "Zur Erläuterung von Jes. 5, 1-7," AFO 4 (1927) : 209-10.

Bergmeier, R. "Zum Ausdruck עצת רשעם in Ps. 1:1; Hiob [Job] 10:3; 21:16; 22:18," ZAW 79 (1967) : 229-33.

Beyerlin, W. *Die Kulttraditionen Israels in der Verkündigung des Propheten Micha*. Göttingen: Vandenhoeck & Ruprecht, 1959.

Blenkinsopp, J. "Theme and motif in the succession history (II Sam. xi 2 ff.) and the Yahwist corpus," VTS 15 (1966) : 44-57.

Boecker, H. J. *Redeformen des Rechtslebens im Alten Testament*. WMANT, Band 14. Neukirchen-Vluyn: Neukirchener Verlag, 1964.

Boström, G. *Proverbiastudien*. Lund: G. W. K. Gleerup, 1928.

Brunner, H. "Die Weisheitsliteratur," *Handbuch der Orientalistik* I,2 (1952) : 90-110.

Buber, M. *The Prophetic Faith*. "Harper Torchbooks"; New York: Harper & Row, 1960.

Bultmann, R. *History of the Synoptic Tradition*. Trans. from the 3rd German ed. with supplementary material by J. Marsh. New York: Harper & Row, 1963.

Buttrick, G., *et al.* (eds.). *The Interpreter's Dictionary of the Bible*, Vols. I-IV. Nashville: Abingdon Press, 1962.

Cazelles, H. "Les débuts de la sagesse en Israel," *Les Sagesses du Proche-Orient ancien*. Paris: Presses Universitaires de France, 1963, pp. 27-40.

Cersoy, P. "L'Apoloque de la Vigne," RB (1899) : 2-12.

Charles, R. H. (ed.). *The Apocrypha and Pseudepigrapha of the Old Testament* I and II. Oxford: The Clarendon Press, 1913.

Cheyne, T. K. *Introduction to the Book of Isaiah*. London: Adam and Charles Clark, 1895.

Childs, B. S. "The Birth of Moses," JBL 84 (1965) : 109-22.

―――――. *Isaiah and the Assyrian Crisis*. SBT, Second Series, 3. London: SCM Press, 1967.

Clements, R. E. *Prophecy and Covenant*. SBT, no. 43. London: SCM Press, 1965.

Clifford, R. J. "The Use of Hôy in the Prophets," CBQ 28 (1966) : 448-64.

Crenshaw, J. L. "The Influence of the Wise upon Amos," ZAW 79 (1967) : 42-51.

―――――. "Method in Determining Wisdom Influence upon 'Historical' Literature," JBL 88 (1969) : 129-42.

Cross, F. M., Jr. "The Council of Yahweh in Second Isaiah," JNES 12 (1953) : 274-77.

De Boer, P. A. H. "The Counsellor," VTS 3 (1955) : 150-61.

Delitzsch, F. *Biblical Commentary on the Prophecies of Isaiah*. Trans. James Martin. Grand Rapids, Michigan: Eerdmans Publishing Company, 1954.

Delcor, M. "Les attaches littéraires, l'origine et la signification de l'expression biblique 'Prendre à temoin le ciel et la terre,' " VT 16 (1966) : 8-26.

De Orbiso, P. T. "El cántico a la viña del Amado (Is. 5, 1-7) ," EstEcl 34 (1960) : 715-31.

Dillmann, A. *Der Prophet Jesaia*. Leipzig: Verlag S. Hirzel, 1890.

Dodd, C. H. *The Parables of the Kingdom*. New York: Charles Scribner's Sons, 1961.

Donner, H. *Israel unter den Völkern. Die Stellung der klassischen Propheten des 8. Jahrhunderts v. Chr. zur Aussenpolitik der Könige von Israel und Juda*. VTS 11 (1964) .

――――. "Die soziale Botschaft der Propheten im Lichte der Gesellschaftsordnung in Israel," *Oriens Antiquus* 2 (1963) : 229-45.

Drubbel, A. "Le Conflit entre la Sagesse Profane et la Sagesse Religieuse. Contribution à l'Etude des Origines de la Littérature Sapientiale en Israel," *Biblica* 17 (1936) : 45-70, 407-26.

Duesberg, H., and Fransen, I. *Les Scribes Inspires*. 2nd rev. ed. Maredsous, 1966.

Duhm, B. *Das Buch Jesaia*. "Göttinger Handkommentar zum Alten Testament," ed. W. Nowack. Göttingen: Vandenhoeck & Ruprecht, 1922.

Dürr, L. *Das Erziehungswesen im Alten Testament und im antiken Orient*. MVAG 36,2. Leipzig, 1932.

Eichrodt, W. *Der Heilige in Israel*. "Die Botschaft des Alten Testaments," Band 17,1. Stuttgart: Calwer Verlag, 1960.

Eissfeldt, O. *Der Maschal im Alten Testament*. BZAW 24. Giessen: Verlag Alfred Töpelmann, 1913.

Elliger, K. *Kleine Schriften zum Alten Testament*. "Theologische Bücherei," Band 32. München: Chr. Kaiser Verlag, 1966.

Ewald, H. *Die Propheten des Alten Bundes*, Band I. Göttingen: Vandenhoeck & Ruprecht, 1867.

Farr, G. "The Language of Amos, Popular or Cultic?" VT 16 (1966) : 312-24.

Fensham, F. C. "Widow, Orphan, and the Poor in Ancient Near Eastern Legal and Wisdom Literature," JNES 21 (1962) : 129-39.

Fey, R. *Amos und Jesaia*. WMANT, Band 12. Neukirchen-Vluyn: Neukirchener Verlag, 1963.

Fichtner, J. *Die altorientalische Weisheit in ihrer israelitisch-jüdischen Ausprägung*. BZAW 62. Giessen: Alfred Töpelmann, 1933.

――――. *Gottes Weisheit: Gesammelte Studien zum Alten Testament*. "Arbeiten zur Theologie," 2. Reihe, Band 3. Stuttgart: Calwer Verlag, 1965.

――――. "Jahwes Plan in der Botschaft des Jesaja," ZAW (1951) : 16-33.

――――. "Jesaja unter den Weisen," ThLZ 74 (1949) , cols. 75-80.

Fischer, J. *Das Buch Isaias* I. Bonn: Peter Hanstein, 1937.

Fohrer, G. "Altes Testament—'Amphiktyonie' und 'Bund'?" ThLZ 91 (1966) , cols. 801-16, 893-903.

————. *Das Buch Jesaia.* "Zürcher Bibelkommentare." Zürich-Stuttgart: Zwingli Verlag, 1960.

————. "Jes. 1 als Zusammenfassung der Verkündigung Jesajas," ZAW 74 (1962) : 251-68.

————. "Neuere Literatur zur alttestamentlichen Prophetie," ThR NF 19 (1951) : 277-346; 20 (1952) : 193-271, 295-361.

————. "Some Remarks on Modern Interpretation of the Prophets," JBL 80 (1961) : 309-19.

————. "σωφία κτλ., B. Altes Testament," TWNT 7 (1964) : 476-96.

————. *Studien zur alttestamentlichen Prophetie* (1949-1965) . BZAW 99. Berlin: Alfred Töpelmann, 1967.

Fullerton, K. "The Problem of Isaiah, Chapter 10," AJSL 34 (1918) : 170-84.

Funk, R. W. *Language, Hermeneutic, and Word of God.* New York: Harper & Row, 1966.

Gemser, B. "The Instructions of 'Onchsheshonqy," VTS 7 (1959) : 102-28.

————. "The *rib*—or controversy—pattern in Hebrew mentality," VTS 3 (1955) : 120-37.

————. *Sprüche Salomos.* HAT 16. Tübingen: J. C. B. Mohr (Paul Siebeck) , 1963.

Gerstenberger, E. "Covenant and Commandment," JBL 84 (1965) : 38-51.

————. Review of D. J. McCarthy's *Treaty and Covenant.* JBL 83 (1964) : 198-99.

————. Review of W. Richter's *Recht und Ethos. Versuch einer Ortung des weisheitlichen Mahnspruches.* JBL 86 (1967) : 489-91.

————. *Wesen und Herkunft des "apodiktischen Rechts."* WMANT, Band 20. Neukirchen-Vluyn: Neukirchener Verlag, 1965.

————. "The Woe-Oracles of the Prophets," JBL 81 (1962) : 249-63.

————. "Zur alttestamentlichen Weisheit," VuF (1968) : 28-44.

Gese, H. *Lehre und Wirklichkeit in der alten Weisheit.* Tübingen: J. C. B. Mohr, 1958.

————. "Weisheit," RGG 3rd ed. VI (1962) : 1574-77.

————. "Weisheitsdichtung," RGG 3rd ed. (1962) : 1577-81.

Gesenius, W. *Jesaia.* Leipzig: Fried. Christ. Wilh. Vogel, 1821.

Good, E. M. *Irony in the Old Testament.* Philadelphia: The Westminster Press, 1965.

Gordon, E. I. *Sumerian Proverbs: Glimpses of Everyday Life in Ancient Mesopotamia.* University of Pennsylvania, Philadelphia: The University Museum, 1959.

Gottwald, N. K. *All the Kingdoms of the Earth: Israelite Prophecy and International Relations in the Ancient Near East.* New York: Harper & Row, 1964.

Gray, G. B. *A Critical and Exegetical Commentary on the Book of*

Isaiah (I-XXVII). "The International Critical Commentary," eds. S. R. Driver, A. Plummer, and C. A. Briggs. Edinburgh: T. & T. Clark, 1912.

Gressmann, H. *Israels Spruchweisheit im Zusammenhang der Weltliteratur*. "Alte Kulturen im Lichte neuer Forschung," VI. Berlin: Karl Curtius, 1925.

Gunkel, H. *Die Propheten*. Göttingen: Vandenhoeck & Ruprecht, 1917.

Hammershaimb, E. "On the Ethics of Old Testament Prophets," VTS 7 (1959) : 75-101.

Harrington, W. "The Wisdom of Israel," IrTQ xxx (1963) : 311-25.

Harvey, J. "Le 'Rîb-Pattern,' réquisitoire prophétique sue la rupture de l'alliance," *Biblica* 43 (1962) : 172-96.

Herntrich, V. *Der Prophet Jesaia*. ATD. Göttingen: Vandenhoeck & Ruprecht, 1950.

Herrmann, S. *Die prophetischen Heilserwartungen im Alten Testament*. Stuttgart: W. Kohlhammer Verlag, 1965.

————. "Prophetie in Israel und Ägypten. Recht und Grenze eines Vergleichs," VTS 9 (1963) : 47-65.

Hesse, F. "Wurzelt die prophetische Gerichtsrede im israelitischen Kultus?" ZAW 65 (1953) : 45-53.

Hillers, D. R. *Treaty-Curses and the Old Testament Prophets*. "Biblica et Orientalia," no. 16. Rome: Pontifical Biblical Institute, 1964.

Holladay, W. L. "Isa. 3:10-11: An Archaic Wisdom Passage," VT 18 (1968) : 481-87.

Hubbard, D. A. "The Wisdom Movement and Israel's Covenant Faith," *The Tyndale Bulletin* (1966), pp. 3-33.

Huffmon, H. B. "The Covenant Lawsuit in the Prophets," JBL 78 (1959) : 285-95.

Irwin, J. R. "The Revelation of עצה in the Old Testament." Unpublished Ph.D. Dissertation, Drew University, 1965.

Janzen, W. "'Ašrê in the Old Testament," HTR 58 (1965) : 216-26.

Jeremias, J. *The Parables of Jesus*. Trans. S. H. Hooke. New York: Charles Scribner's Sons, 1963.

Johnson, A. R. *The Cultic Prophet in Ancient Israel*. 2nd ed. (revised). Cardiff: University of Wales Press, 1962.

Jolles, A. *Einfache Formen*. Tübingen: Max Niemeyer Verlag, 1958.

Junker, H. "Die literarische Art von Is. 5, 1-7," *Biblica* 40 (1959) : 259-66.

Kaiser, O. *Der Prophet Jesaia, Kap. 1-12*. ATD 17. Göttingen: Vandenhoeck & Ruprecht, 1960.

Kayatz, C. *Studien zu Proverbien 1-9*. WMANT, Band 22. Neukirchen-Vluyn: Neukirchener Verlag, 1966.

Kingsbury, E. C. "The Prophets and the Council of Yahweh," JBL 83 (1964) : 279-87.

Knierim, R. *Die Hauptbegriffe für Sünde im Alten Testament.* Gütersloh: Gütersloher Verlagshaus Gerd Mohn, 1965.

———. "The Vocation of Isaiah," VT 18 (1968) : 47-68.

Koch, K. "Gibt es ein Vergeltungsdogma im Alten Testament?" ZThK 52 (1955) : 1-42.

König, E. *Das Buch Jesaja.* Gütersloh: C. Bertelsmann, 1926.

Kramer, S. N. *History Begins at Sumer.* London: Thames and Hudson, 1958.

———. *Sumerian Literary Texts from Nippur: The Annual of the American Schools of Oriental Research,* Vol. XXIII (1943-44). New Haven, 1944.

Kraus, H. J. "Die prophetische Botschaft gegen das soziale Unrecht Israels," EvTh 15 (1955) : 295-307.

———. *Psalmen.* BKAT XV. Neukirchen: Kreis Moers, 1960.

Lambert, W. G. *Babylonian Wisdom Literature.* Oxford: The Clarendon Press, 1960.

LeClant, J. *et al. Les Sagesses du Proche-Orient ancien.* Paris: Presses Universitaires de France, 1963.

Liebreich, L. J. "The Parable Taken from the Farmer's Labors in Is. XXVIII, 23-29" (Hebr.) , *Tarbiz* XXIV/2 (1955) : 126-28. (English Summary in *Internationale Zeitschriftenschau für Bibelwissenschaft und Grenzgebiete,* Band IV, Heft 1-2 [Düsseldorff: Patmos Verlag, 1955/56].)

Lindblom, J. *Prophecy in Ancient Israel.* Oxford: Basil Blackwell, 1963.

———. "Wisdom in the Old Testament Prophets," VTS 3 (1955) : 192-204.

Loewenclau, Ilse von, "Zur Auslegung von Jesaja 1,2-3," EvTh 6 (1966) : 294-308.

Malfroy, J. "Sagesse et Loi dans le Deutéronomie," VT 15 (1965) : 49-65.

Marshall, R. J. "The Structure of Isaiah 1-12," *Biblical Research* VII (1962) : 19-33.

Marti, K. *Das Buch Jesaja.* "Kurzer Handkommentar zum Alten Testament." Tübingen: J. C. B. Mohr (Paul Siebeck) , 1900.

Martin-Achard, R. "Sagesse de Dieu et Sagesse humaine chez Esaie," *Maqqel Shaqedh, Hommage à Wilhelm Vischer.* Montpellier, 1960, pp. 137-44.

McCarthy, D. J., S.J. *Treaty and Covenant.* "Analecta Biblica," 21. Rome: Pontifical Biblical Institute, 1963.

McKane, W. *Prophets and Wise Men.* SBT no 44. London: SCM Press, 1965.

Mendenhall, G. *Law and Covenant in Israel and the Ancient Near East.* Pittsburgh, Pa.: The Biblical Colloquium, 1955.

Montgomery, J. W. "Wisdom as Gift. The Wisdom Concept in Relation to Biblical Messianism," *Interpretation* 16 (1962) : 43-57.

Moran, W. L. "Some Remarks on the Song of Moses," *Biblica* 43 (1962) : 317-27.

Mowinckel, S. "Psalms and Wisdom," VTS 3 (1955) : 205-24.

Muilenburg, J. "The 'Office' of the Prophet in Ancient Israel," *The Bible in Modern Scholarship*, ed. P. H. Hyatt. Nashville: Abingdon Press, 1965.

Murphy, R. "Assumptions and Problems in Old Testament Wisdom Research," CBQ 29 (1967) : 407-18.

Noth, M. "Die Bewährung von Salomos 'göttlicher Weisheit,' " VTS 3 (1955) : 225-37.

―――. *The Laws in the Pentateuch and Other Studies*. Trans. D. R. Ap-Thomas. Philadelphia: Fortress Press, 1967.

―――, and Thomas, D. W. (eds.) . *Wisdom in Israel and the Ancient Near East*. VTS 3. Leiden: E. J. Brill, 1955.

Orelli, C. von. *The Prophecies of Isaiah*. Trans. J. S. Banks. Edinburgh: T. & T. Clark, 1889.

Östborn, G. *Torah in the Old Testament*. Lund: Haakon Ohlsson, 1945.

Pezzella, S. "La parabola della vigna (Is. 5,1-7) ," *Bibbia e Oriente* 5 (1963) : 5-8.

Pfeiffer, R. H. *Introduction to the Old Testament*. New York: Harper & Bros., 1948.

―――. "Wisdom and Vision in the Old Testament," ZAW 52 (1934) : 93-101.

Porteous, N. W. "The Prophets and the Problem of Continuity," *Israel's Prophetic Heritage*, eds. B. W. Anderson and W. Harrelson. New York: Harper & Bros., 1962, pp. 11-25.

―――. "Royal Wisdom," VTS 3 (1955) : 247-61.

Priest, J. F. "Where Is Wisdom to Be Placed?" JBR 31 (1963) : 275-82.

Pritchard, J. B. (ed.) . *Ancient Near Eastern Texts Relating to the Old Testament*. 2nd ed. Princeton, New Jersey: Princeton University Press, 1955.

Procksch, O. *Jesaja I*. KAT IX. Leipzig: A. Deichert, 1930.

Rad, G. von. "Die ältere Weisheit Israels," KuD 2 (1956) : 54-72.

―――. "The Joseph Narrative and Ancient Wisdom," *The Problem of the Hexateuch and Other Essays*, trans. E. W. Trueman Dicken. New York: McGraw Hill, 1966, pp. 292-300.

―――. *Die Josephgeschichte*. "Biblische Studien," Heft 5. Neukirchen: Neukirchener Verlag, 1964.

―――. *Old Testament Theology* I, trans. D. M. G. Stalker. New York: Harper & Row, 1965.

————. *Old Testament Theology* II, trans. D. M. G. Stalker. New York: Harper & Row, 1965.

————. "Das Werk Jahwes," *Studia Biblica et Semitica,* eds. W. C. van Unnik and A. S. van der Woude. Wageningen: H. Veenman, 1966, pp. 290-98.

Rankin, O. S. *Israel's Wisdom Literature.* Edinburgh: T. & T. Clark, 1936.

Ranston, H. *The Old Testament Wisdom Books and Their Teaching.* London: The Epworth Press, 1930.

Reventlow, H. G. *Das Amt des Propheten bei Amos.* FRLANT 20. Göttingen: Vandenhoeck & Ruprecht, 1962.

Richter, W. *Recht und Ethos. Versuch einer Ortung des weisheitlichen Mahnspruches.* "Studien am Alten und Neuen Testament," XV. München: Kösel Verlag, 1966.

————. *Traditionsgeschichtliche Untersuchungen zum Richterbuch.* "Bonner Biblische Beiträge," 18, eds. Johannes Botterweck and Karl Th. Schäfer. Bonn: Peter Hanstein Verlag, 1963.

Rignell, L. G. "Isaiah, Chapter I. Some exegetical remarks with special reference of the relationship between the text and the book of Deuteronomy," StTh 11 (1957), pp. 140-58.

Robertson, E. "Isaiah, Chapter I," ZAW 52 (1934) : 231-36.

Robinson, H. W. "The Council of Yahweh," JTS 45 (1944) : 151-57.

————. *Inspiration and Revelation in the Old Testament.* Oxford: The Clarendon Press, 1946.

Rowley, H. H. "The Nature of Prophecy in the Light of Recent Study," HTR 38 (1945) : 1-38.

Rylaarsdam, J. C. *Revelation in Jewish Wisdom Literature.* Chicago: University of Chicago Press, 1946.

Saebö, M. "Zur Traditionsgeschichte von Jesaja 8:9-10," ZAW 35 (1964) : 132-44.

Sanders, J. A. *Suffering as Divine Discipline in the Old Testament and Post-Biblical Judaism.* Rochester: Colgate Rochester Divinity School Bulletin, XXVIII, 1955.

Schmid, H. H. *Wesen und Geschichte der Weisheit.* BZAW 101. Berlin: Alfred Töpelmann, 1966.

Scott, R. B. Y. *The Book of Isaiah,* Vol. 5: *The Interpreter's Bible.* Nashville: Abingdon Press, 1956.

————. *Proverbs. Ecclesiastes.* "The Anchor Bible," Vol. 18. New York: Doubleday & Co., 1965.

————. "Solomon and the Beginnings of Wisdom in Israel," VTS 3 (1955) : 262-70.

Simon, U. "The Poor Man's Ewe-Lamb. An Example of a Juridical Parable," *Biblica* 48 (1967) : 207-42.

Skinner, J. *Isaiah.* Cambridge: The University Press, 1905.

Skladny, U. *Die ältesten Spruchsammlungen in Israel.* Göttingen: Vandenhoeck & Ruprecht, 1962.

Smith, G. A. *The Book of Isaiah.* "The Expositor's Bible." London: Hodder and Stoughton, 1889.

Talmon, S. " 'Wisdom' in the Book of Esther," VT 13 (1963) : 419-55.

Terrien, S. "Amos and Wisdom," *Israel's Prophetic Heritage,* eds. B. W. Anderson and W. Harrelson. New York: Harper & Bros., 1962, pp. 108-15.

Thexton, S. C. "A Note to Isaiah XXVIII, 25 and 28," VT 2 (1952) : 81-83.

Thompson, J. M. "The Form and Function of Proverbs in Ancient Israel." Unpublished Doctoral thesis, Vanderbilt University, 1965.

Toombs, L. E. "O. T. Theology and the Wisdom Literature," JBR 23 (1955) : 193-96.

Vriezen, T. C. "Essentials of the Theology of Isaiah," *Israel's Prophetic Heritage,* eds. B. W. Anderson and W. Harrelson. New York: Harper & Bros., 1962, pp. 128-46.

Waldow, E. von. *Der traditionsgeschichtliche Hintergrund der prophetischen Gerichtsreden.* BZAW 85. Berlin: Alfred Töpelmann, 1963.

Wanke, G. "אוי und הוֹי," ZAW 78 (1966) : 215-18.

Westermann, C. *Forschung am Alten Testament.* "Theologische Bücherei," 24. München: Chr. Kaiser Verlag, 1964.

——. *Grundformen prophetischer Rede.* Zweite, erweiterte Auflage: BEvTh, Band 31. München: Chr. Kaiser Verlag, 1964.

Whybray, R. N. *Wisdom in Proverbs.* SBT, no. 45. London: SCM Press, 1965.

——. *The Succession Narrative: A Study of II Samuel 9-20, I Kings 1 and 2.* SBT, Second series, 9. London: SCM Press, 1968.

Wildberger, H. *Jesaja.* BKAT X. Neukirchen-Vluyn: Neukirchener Verlag, 1966 ff.

——. "Jesaja's Verständnis der Geschichte," VTS 9 (1963) : 83-117.

——. "Die Thronnamen des Messias, Jes. 9: 5b," TZ 76 (1960) : 314-32.

Wilder, A. N. *The Language of the Gospel: Early Christian Rhetoric.* New York: Harper & Row, 1964.

Williams, J. G. "The Alas-Oracles of the Eighth Century Prophets," HUCA 38 (1967) : 75-92.

Wolff, H. W. *Amos' geistige Heimat.* WMANT, Band 18. Neukirchen-Vluyn: Neukirchener Verlag, 1964.

——. *Dodekapropheten I. Hosea.* BKAT, Band XIV/1. Neukirchen: Kreis Moers, 1961.

——. *Frieden ohne Ende. Jes. 7,1-17 und 9,1-6 ausgelegt.* "Biblische Studien," 35. Neukirchen: Neukirchener Verlag, 1962.

——. *Gesammelte Studien zum Alten Testament.* "Theologische

Bücherei," Band 22. München: Chr. Kaiser Verlag, 1964.

Wright, G. E. Isaiah. "Layman's Bible Commentaries." London: SCM Press, 1964.

Würthwein, E. "Amos-Studien," ZAW 62 (1950) : 10-52.

———, and Kaiser, O., eds. Tradition und Situation: Studien zur alttestamentlichen Prophetie. Göttingen: Vandenhoeck & Ruprecht, 1963.

———. "Der Ursprung der prophetischen Gerichtsrede," ZThK 49 (1952) : 1-16.

Yeivin, S. "Social, Religious, and Cultural Trends in Jerusalem under the Davidic Dynasty," VT 3 (1953) : 149-66.

Zimmerli, W. Gottes Offenbarung: Gesammelte Aufsätze. "Theologische Bücherei," Band 19. München: Chr. Kaiser Verlag, 1963.

———. The Law and the Prophets: A Study of the Meaning of the Old Testament, trans. R. E. Clements. Oxford: Basil Blackwell, 1965.

———. "Zur Struktur der alttestamentlichen Weisheit," ZAW 51 (1933) . 177-204.

Index of
Biblical References

165

Index of
Subjects and Authors